Contents

Contents

Dear Teddy Bear Lovers,

As we all know Teddies are very special in so many ways, for the feelings they evoke when looking at a bear that "talks" to you, for the joy one experiences when creating a new bear and for the sheer pleasure of owning as many different and special bears as possible.

In this book we introduce you to the wonderful world of KNITTED BEARS. There are many exquisite yarns available in the world today, which when knitted up, can make exciting, beautiful bears. The possibilities are limitless....luxurious bears in glamorous fancy yarns or simpler bears in less expensive yarns, but still interesting textures and fibres. Whichever yarn you choose, you will have great fun creating these wonderful knitted bears. As you knit and start assembling the pieces, the bears begin assuming their characters, coming to life, and so the bear love affair begins!

I know that you are going to enjoy knitting the bears in this book as much as we have enjoyed creating them. I wish you many hours of happy teddy bear crafting and encourage you to be as adventurous as you can, as beautiful yarns make beautiful bears!

Sharon Farr

General Instructions and Bear Making Techniques

Materials

The following basic requirements are needed for successful bear making. More specific materials will be listed in each individual bear pattern.

- Knitting needles
- Yarn
- Eyes
- Noses (felt or plastic)
- Strong thread to attach eyes
- Sewing needle
- Long Doll needle (for sew-in eyes)
- Glass headed pins
- Embroidery thread
- Embroidery needles
- Small sharp scissor
- Long nose pliers
- Polyester stuffing
- Selection of ribbon

Abbreviations

alt = alternate; **beg** = begin(ning); **C4F(B)** = Cable 4 front(back), sl next 2sts onto cn and leave at front(back) of work, k2, then k2 from cn; **cn** = cable needle; **cont** = continue; **dc** = double crochet; **dec** = decrease(ing); **foll(s)** = follow(s)ing; **g st** = garter stitch; **inc(s)** = increase(s)ing thus, work into the front and back of the stitch; **k** = knit; **k(p)w** = knit (purl) wise; **patt(s)** = pattern(s); **p** = purl; **rem** = remain(ing); **rep** = repeat; **rev st st** = reverse stocking stitch, purlside as right side; **R(W)S** = right (wrong) side; **R(W)SF** = right (wrong) side facing; **R(W)SR** = right (wrong) side row; **RW** = ribwise; **st(s)** = stitch(es); **st st** = stocking stitch; **sl** = slip; **SKPO** = slip one, knit one, pass slipped stitch over; **tog** = together; **yfd** = yarn forward.
A, B or **C** refers to different colour yarns used (see under materials).

Stitches Used

STOCKING STITCH: **1st row**: K. **2nd row**: P. Rep 1st and 2nd rows.
GARTER STITCH: Every row: K.
RIB: K1, p1.
REVERSE STOCKING STITCH: **1st row**: P. **2nd row**: K. Rep 1st and 2nd rows.

SWISS DARNING IS AN EXCITING KNITTING CONCEPT. EASIER THAN FAIRISLE, IT IS CREATIVE AND GIVES A NEATER OVERALL EFFECT.
This embroidery technique is sometimes called "The Duplicate Stitch", doing precisely what the name implies - duplicating the outline of each stocking stitch. The technique itself is not difficult (see diagrams below); but to keep embroidered stitches to the same tension as the knitted garment the technique needs to be practised on a knitted square until perfected.

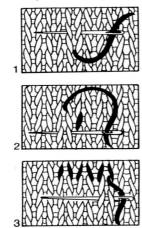

Tension

Tension is vitally important in knitting. In order to achieve the best result possible, take the time to check your tension, whether you are using the yarn specified or most especially if using a yarn other than is stated in the pattern. If you choose a substitute yarn, it must be of the same thickness and texture as the yarn originally used if you want your bear to look similar to the bear in the picture (see table below for a general guide to tension and thickness of different yarns). The tensions stated in the patterns are for knitters with average tension, if your tension is too loose or too tight than that required, the following rule will help you.
IF THERE ARE TOO FEW STS ON TEST SWATCH, USE THINNER NEEDLES; IF THERE ARE TOO MANY STS, USE THICKER NEEDLES.

Weight	Sts per 10cm/4"	Symbol
Fine	29-32sts	✧
Light	25-28sts	☆
Medium	21-24sts	✳
Heavy Medium	17-20sts	✶
Hunky	13-16sts	✷
Extra Hunky	9-12sts	✸

Note:
1. See each pattern for the symbol pertaining to yarn weight used.
2. See page 59 for yarns, tensions and weights of South African yarns used in these patterns.

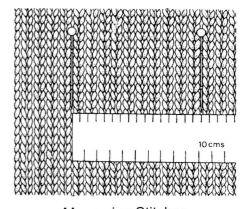

Measuring Stitches

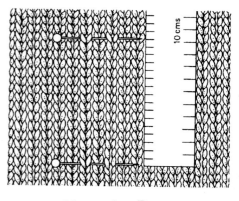

Measuring Rows

Making Up

When sewing up your knitted pieces it is very important that you use the back stitch method (see diagram). Keeping seams even and securing the thread firmly at the beginning and end of each seam, sew all pieces using a firm back stitch. This method ensures nice even seams with no holes.

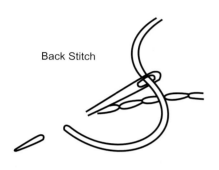

Back Stitch

The sewing up of your bear is worth taking time and care over, as bad sewing up will result in an untidy looking bear. Avoid unsightly threads by threading your ends back through the stuffing in your bear. Legs and arms can be attached in two ways:

FIXED
Stuff firmly, sew closed and attach in position to the body.

MOVABLE
Stuff each section firmly and sew closed. Make a mark on each side of the body in the position you want to place the arms or legs. Take a long doll needle threaded with dental floss or a very strong thread and insert in right hand socket position, take the needle through to the left side, make a small stitch, bring the needle back to the right side of the body, make a small stitch and repeat the operation ending with a small x in each socket. Pull the threads tightly causing the sockets to indent. Fasten off. Position arm or leg into indentation. Using a pin mark intended sewing position on inside of arm or leg for attachment to body. With another length of thread sew arm or leg in place by taking needle through body, into arm or leg at marker, back through body, into second arm or leg at marker, back through body. Repeat the action. When the arms or legs are firmly attached, fasten off.

Eyes

The eyes you choose for your bear is a matter of personal preference depending on the look you want to create. Safety eyes (plastic eyes with a plastic backing washer) are attached before the head is stuffed and are recommended if the bear is intended for small children. Glass eyes with wire loops are most popular with bear artists and are attached after the head is stuffed. See diagrams below for two methods of attaching eyes.

1. Using a long doll needle insert your yarn at the base of the back neck, bring your needle out in the position you want the eye, thread the eye onto the needle positioning the wire loop between a knitted stitch, insert the needle into the next stitch and take back out at the base of the neck a couple of millimetres from the first thread. Tie off, then thread the ends into the head through the stuffing. Repeat for second eye.

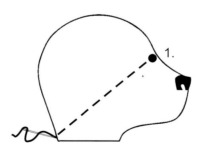

2. Insert the needle at the base of the centre back neck and bring out in the position you want your eye. Thread the eye as previously mentioned, then take your needle out through the muzzle to exit at the opposite eye. Now thread the second eye onto your needle and bring the yarn out a couple of millimetres from where you began. Tie off, then thread the ends into the head through the stuffing.

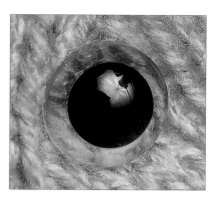

Plastic Eye

Glass Eye

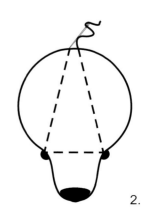

Lidded Eye

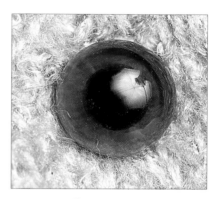

Nose and Mouth

There are many different sizes, textures and shapes of plastic noses available. These noses are attached before the head is stuffed in the same way as safety eyes. It is important to ensure that the stem of the plastic nose is inserted in the centre of the join in the muzzle (see picture). If not, your nose will be slightly off-centre and your face will not look right.

Inserting a plastic nose in centre of seam joins

Plastic Nose

Flocked Nose

Felt Nose

Most bear artists prefer embroidering the nose as many shapes and sizes can be achieved. Embroidering a nose is not easy and requires practise. It is a critical part of construction therefore take the time to get it right. A template of leather or felt can be cut out in the desired shape and used as a guideline for the embroidery. The secret to a good embroidered nose is in the stitch tension which should be kept firm and even. Once your nose is ready you can begin to embroider the mouth. Bring the needle out at the centre base of the nose and embroider the mouth using straight stitches in a shape that suits your bear. See diagrams (right) for some nose and mouth shapes.

Ears

Close the cast on edges of each ear using ladder stitch (see diagram). Experiment with different positions for the ears, once you are happy pin your ears in place and ladder stitch to the head. Take time to ensure a neat finish by ensuring that the ears are secured tightly at each end. When complete, thread all loose threads into the stuffing of the head.

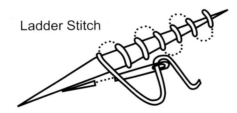

Ladder Stitch

The position of the ears, eyes and nose will determine the final expression on your bear's face, so take time to experiment with different positions in order to achieve exactly the face that you are looking for.

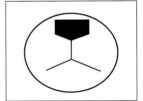

NEEDLE SIZES

Metric	15	9	7½	7	6½	6	5½	5	4½	4	3¾	3¼	3	mm
English	-	00	1	2	3	4	5	6	7	8	9	10	11	
American	19	13	11	-	10½	10	9	8	7	6	5	4	-	

Oscar

MATERIALS:
VELLUTO
150g colour of your choice
One pair 12mm amber glass eyes
One 25mm black plastic nose
Oddments of black yarn for
embroidery
Length of ribbon
Polyester stuffing
One pair 3,75mm knitting needles.

MEASUREMENTS:
Oscar measures 32cm(12½ins)
sitting and 50cm(19¾ ins) standing.

TENSION:
SAVE TIME, TAKE TIME, CHECK TENSION.
22sts and 30 rows = 10cm(4 ins) over
stocking stitch using 3,75mm needles.

Body

Begin at bottom
Using the appropriate needles cast on
16sts.
1st row: K.
2nd row: SHAPE BODY: P, inc into
first 4sts, p2sts, inc into next 4sts,
p2sts, inc into last 4sts = 28sts.
3rd row: K, inc into first 2sts, k10sts,
inc into next 4sts, k10sts, inc into last
2sts = 36sts.
4th row: P, inc into first 2sts, p14sts,
inc into next 4sts, p14sts, inc into last
2sts = 44sts.
5th row: K, inc into first st, k20sts, inc
into next 2sts, k20sts, inc into last st =
48sts.
6th row: P, inc into first st, p22sts, inc
into next 2sts, p22sts, inc into last st =
52sts.
7th row: K, inc 1 st at each end of row
= 54sts.
8th row: P26sts, inc into next 2sts,
p26sts = 56sts.
9th row: K, inc 1 st at each end of row
= 58sts.
10th row: P28sts, inc into next 2sts,
p28sts = 60sts.
11th row: K, inc 1 st at each end of
row = 62sts.
12th row: P30sts, inc into next 2sts,
p30sts = 64sts.
13th to 15th row: Inc 1 st at each end
of next and foll alt row = 68sts.
16th row: P.
17th row: K33sts, inc into next 2sts,
k33sts = 70sts.

18th to 20th row: Work in st st.
21st row: K, inc 1 st at each end of
row = 72sts.
22nd to 30th row: Work in st st.
31st row: K, dec 1 st (= work 2tog) at
each end of row = 70sts.
32nd to 34th row: Work in st st.
35th row: K, dec 1 st at each end of
row = 68sts.
36th row: P32sts, (p2tog) twice,
p32sts = 66sts.
37th to 41st row: Work in st st.
42nd row: P31sts, (p2tog) twice,
p31sts = 64sts.
43rd to 47th row: Work in st st.
48th row: P30sts, (p2tog) twice,
p30sts = 62sts.
49th to 51st row: Work in st st.
52nd row: P29sts, (p2tog) twice,
p29sts = 60sts.
53rd to 55th row: Work in st st.
56th row: P28sts, (p2tog) twice,
p28sts = 58sts.
57th row: K.
58th row: P27sts, (p2tog) twice,
p27sts = 56sts.
59th row: K.
60th row: P2tog, p24sts, (p2tog)
twice, p24sts, p2tog = 52sts.
61st to 63rd row: Work in st st.
64th row: P2tog, p22sts, (p2tog)
twice, p22sts, p2tog = 48sts.
65th row: K.
66th row: P22sts, (p2tog) twice,
p22sts = 46sts.
67th row: K.
68th row: P21sts, (p2tog) twice,
p21sts = 44sts.
69th and 70th row: Dec 1 st at each
end of next and foll row = 40sts.
71st row: K.
72nd row: P, dec 1 st at each end of
row = 38sts.
73rd row: K13sts, (k2tog) 6 times,
k13sts = 32sts.
74th row: P2tog, p2sts, (p2tog) 12
times, p2sts, p2tog = 18sts.
75th row: (K3tog) 6 times = 6sts.
76th row: P.
77th row: (K2tog) 3 times = 3sts.
78th row: P3tog, fasten off.

Head

Begin at neck edge
Using the appropriate needles cast on
40sts.
1st row: K.
2nd row: SHAPE HEAD: P17sts, inc
into next st, p4sts, inc into next st,
p17sts = 42sts.

3rd to 5th row: Work in st st.
6th row: P18sts, inc into next 2sts,
p2sts, inc into next 2sts, p18sts =
46sts.
7th row: K, inc 1 st at each end of row
= 48sts.
8th row: P.
9th row: K, inc 1 st at each end of row
= 50sts.
10th row: P21sts, inc into next 2sts,
p4sts, inc into next 2sts, p21sts =
54sts.
11th row: K, inc 1 st at each end of
row = 56sts.
12th row: P.
13th row: K, inc 1 st at each end of
row = 58sts.
14th row: P, inc into first st, p24sts,
inc into next st, p6sts, inc into next st,
p24sts, inc into last st = 62sts.
15th row: K, inc into first st, k24sts,
inc into next st, k10sts, inc into next st,
k24sts, inc into last st = 66sts.
16th and 17th row: Inc 1 st at each
end of next and foll row = 70sts.
18th row: P30sts, inc into next st,
p8sts, inc into next st, p30sts = 72sts.
19th row: K, inc 1 st at each end of
row = 74sts.
20th row: P.
21st row: K, inc 1 st at each end of
row = 76sts.
22nd row: P32sts, inc into next st,
p10sts, inc into next st, p32sts = 78sts.
23rd to 27th row: Work in st st.
28th row: P32sts, inc into next st,
p12sts, inc into next st, p32sts = 80sts.
29th to 31st row: Work in st st.
32nd row: P30sts, p2tog, p16sts,
p2tog, p30sts = 78sts.
33rd row: K.
34th row: P30sts, inc into next st,
p16sts, inc into next st, p30sts = 80sts.
35th row: K2tog, k27sts, k2tog,
k18sts, k2tog, k27sts, k2tog = 76sts.
36th and 37th row: Cast off 7sts at
beg of each row = 62sts.
38th row: Cast off 2sts, p17sts,
p2tog, p18sts, p2tog, p20sts = 58sts.
39th row: Cast off 2sts, k to end =
56sts.
40th row: P2tog, p15sts, p2tog,
p18sts, p2tog, p15sts, p2tog = 52sts.
41st row: K, dec 1 st (= work 2tog) at
each end of row = 50sts.
42nd row: P2tog, p12sts, p2tog,
p18sts, p2tog, p12sts, p2tog = 46sts.
43rd row: K2tog, k10sts, k2tog,
k18sts, k2tog, k10sts, k2tog = 42sts.
44th row: P2tog, p8sts, p2tog,
p18sts, p2tog, p8sts, p2tog = 38sts.

45th row: Cast off 3sts, k4sts, k2tog, k18sts, k2tog, k8sts = 33sts.

46th row: Cast off 3sts, p to end = 30sts.

47th and 48th row: Cast off 6sts at beg of each row = 18sts.

49th to 53rd row: Work in st st.

54th row: P, dec 1 st at each end of row = 16sts.

55th to 57th row: Work in st st.

58th to 62nd row: Dec 1 st at each end of next and foll alt rows = 10sts.

63rd to 65th row: Work in st st.

66th row: P, dec 1 st at each end of row = 8sts.

67th to 73rd row: Work in st st.

74th row: P, dec 1 st at each end of row = 6sts.

75th to 77th row: Work in st st.

78th row: P, dec 1 st at each end of row = 4sts.

79th row: K.
Cast off all sts.

Ears

Make 4
Using the appropriate needles cast on 16sts.

1st to 5th row: Work in st st.

6th row: P, dec 1 st (= work 2tog) at each end of row = 14sts.

7th to 9th row: Work in st st.

10th to 14th row: Dec 1 st at each end of next and foll alt rows = 8sts.

15th row: K, dec 1 st at each end of row = 6sts.
Cast off.

Legs

Both Alike
Using the appropriate needles cast on 52sts.

1st to 5th row: Work in st st.

6th row: SHAPE FOOT: P24sts, (p2tog) twice, p24sts = 50sts.

7th to 9th row: Work in st st.

10th row: P23sts, (p2tog) twice, p23sts = 48sts.

11th to 13th row: Work in st st.

14th row: P20sts, (p2tog) 4 times, p20sts = 44sts.

15th row: K20sts, (k2tog) twice, k20sts = 42sts.

16th row: P15sts, (p2tog) 6 times, p15sts = 36sts.

17th row: K.

18th row: P14sts, (p2tog) 4 times, p14sts = 32sts.

19th row: K.

20th row: P14sts, (p2tog) twice, p14sts = 30sts.

***21st to 30th row: Work in st st.

31st row: K14sts, inc into next 2sts, k14sts = 32sts.

32nd and 33rd row: Work in st st.

34th row: P, inc 1 st at each end of row = 34sts.

35th to 38th row: Work in st st.

39th row: K16sts, inc into next 2sts, k16sts = 36sts.

40th row: P.

41st row: K, inc 1 st at each end of row = 38sts.

42nd to 47th row: Work in st st.

48th row: P, inc 1 st at each end of row = 40sts.

49th row: K.

50th row: P19sts, inc into next 2sts, p19sts = 42sts.

51st to 55th row: Work in st st.

56th row: P, dec 1 st (= work 2tog) at each end of row = 40sts.

57th row: K.

58th row: P18sts, (p2tog) twice, p18sts = 38sts.

59th and 60th row: Work in st st.

61st row: K, dec 1 st at each end of row = 36sts.

62nd row: P16sts, (p2tog) twice, p16sts = 34sts.

63rd row: K2tog, k13sts, (k2tog) twice, k13sts, k2tog = 30sts.

64th row: P, dec 1 st at each end of row = 28sts.

65th row: K2tog, k10sts, (k2tog) twice, k10sts, k2tog = 24sts.

66th row: P2tog, p8sts, (p2tog) twice, p8sts, p2tog = 20sts.

67th row: (K2tog) twice, k to last 4sts, (k2tog) twice = 16sts.

68th row: P2sts, (p2tog) 6 times, p2sts = 10sts.

69th row: K2tog to end = 5sts.

70th row: P2tog, p1, p2tog = 3sts.

71st row: K3tog, fasten off.

Soles

Both Alike

Using the appropriate needles cast on 2sts.

1st row: K.

2nd and 3rd row: Cast on 2sts at beg of each row = 6sts.

4th row: P, inc 1 st at each end of row = 8sts.

5th row: K.

6th row: P, inc 1 st at each end of row = 10sts.

7th row: K.

8th row: P, inc 1 st at each end of row = 12sts.

9th to 24th row: Work in st st.

*25th row: K, dec 1 st at each end of row.

26th row: P*.

27th to 30th row: Rep from * to * twice = 6sts.

31st row: K2tog, k2sts, k2tog = 4sts.

32nd row: (P2tog) twice = 2sts.

33rd row: K2tog, fasten off.

Arms

Both Alike
Using the appropriate needles cast on 8sts.

1st row: K.

2nd row: SHAPE ARM: *P, inc into first 2sts, p1*, rep from * to * once more, inc into last 2sts = 14sts.

3rd row: K, inc into first st, k5sts, inc into next 2sts, k5sts, inc into last st = 18sts.

4th row: P, inc into first st, p7sts, inc into next 2sts, p7sts, inc into last st = 22sts.

5th row: K, inc 1 st at each end of row = 24sts.

6th row: P11sts, inc into next 2sts, p11sts = 26sts.

7th and 8th row: Inc 1 st at each end of next and foll row = 30sts.

9th row: K.

10th to 12th row: Inc 1 st at each end of next and foll alt row = 34sts.

13th row: K.

14th row: P, inc 1 st at each end of row = 36sts.

15th row: K, inc into first st, k15sts, (k2tog) twice, k15sts, inc into last st = 36sts.

16th row: P.

17th row: K16sts, (k2tog) twice, k16sts = 34sts.

18th row: P.

19th row: K, inc 1 st at each end of row = 36sts.

20th row: P16sts, (p2tog) twice, p16sts = 34sts.

21st row: K.

22nd row: P, inc into first st, p14sts, (p2tog) twice, p14sts, inc into last st = 34sts.

23rd row: K15sts, (k2tog) twice, k15sts = 32sts.

24th row: P14sts, (p2tog) twice, p14sts = 30sts.

25th row: K, inc 1 st at each end of row = 32sts.

26th row: P14sts, (p2tog) twice, p14sts = 30sts.

27th to 29th row: Work in st st.

30th row: P, inc into first st, p12sts, (p2tog) twice, p12sts, inc into last st = 30sts.

31st to 37th row: Work in st st.

38th row: P, inc 1 st at each end of row = 32sts.

39th row: K15sts, inc into next 2sts, k15sts = 34sts.

40th to 48th row: Work in st st.

49th row: K16sts, inc into next 2sts, k16sts = 36sts.

50th to 57th row: Work in st st.

58th row: P2tog, p14sts, (p2tog) twice, p14sts, p2tog = 32sts.

59th to 61st row: Work in st st.

62nd row: P2tog, p12sts, (p2tog) twice, p12sts, p2tog = 28sts.

63rd row: K.
64th row: P2tog, p10sts, (p2tog) twice, p10sts, p2tog = 24sts.
65th row: K2tog, k8sts, (k2tog) twice, k8sts, k2tog = 20sts.
66th row: P2tog, p6sts, (p2tog) twice, p6sts, p2tog = 16sts.
67th row: K2tog to end = 8sts.
68th row: P2tog to end = 4sts.
69th row: (K2tog) twice = 2sts.
70th row: P2tog, fasten off.

To Make Up:

Sew all pieces using back stitch (see general instructions). **BODY:** With right sides to inside sew back seam closed leaving an opening for stuffing. Stuff firmly and ladder stitch (see general instructions) the gap closed. **HEAD:** With right sides to inside sew side seams of head gusset (see diagram 1), then muzzle seam (see diagram 2), leaving neck (cast on edge) open. If nose and eyes need to be attached before stuffing, do so now (see general instructions). Stuff head and nose firmly. Using a new thread, run a gathering stitch around neck (cast on edge) of head and pull in tightly. Fasten off. Pin head to body ensuring nose seam and centre front of body are in line. Sew head firmly to body by pressing head down onto the body and sewing, making sure that the head remains straight on the body. The firmer you press the head onto the body, the more stable the head will be.
EARS: With right sides to inside, sew curved edge leaving cast on edge open. Stuff ears very lightly and sew closed using ladder stitch. Pin to head in desired position. Sew firmly to head ensuring neat edges. **LEGS:** Fold in half with right sides to inside, and sew seam leaving an opening for stuffing. Sew sole (RS to inside) into position at base of foot. Turn right side out and stuff legs and feet firmly. Close opening. Pin legs to body in desired position, either for a standing or sitting bear, ensuring that they are equally placed on either side of body. Sew legs firmly to body taking care to sew a fairly large section of leg to the body to ensure firm posture. **ARMS:** Fold in half with right sides to inside, sew seams leaving an opening for stuffing. Turn right side out and stuff firmly. Close opening. Pin arms to body as close to the head as possible ensuring that they are of equal distance on either side of body. Sew firmly to body (arms will drop slightly away from head when complete). Embroider mouth (see general instructions). Tie ribbon around neck.

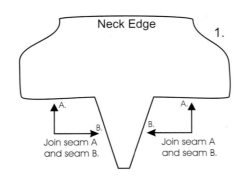

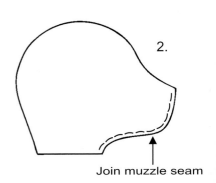

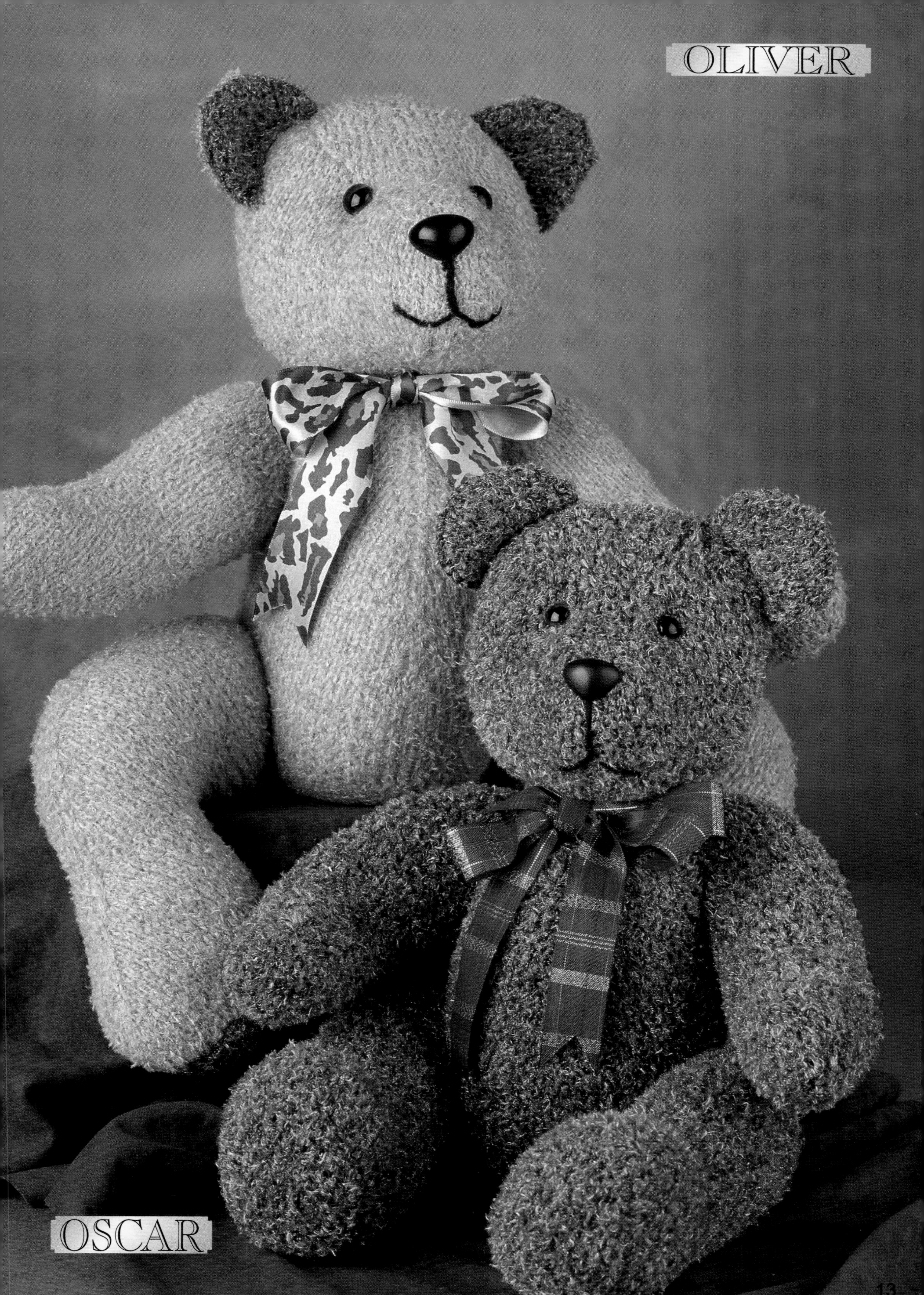
OLIVER
OSCAR

Oliver

MATERIALS:
VELLUTO
150g Sabbia A and 50g Chocolato B
One pair 16mm amber glass eyes
One 30mm black plastic nose
Oddments of black yarn for
embroidery
Polyester stuffing
Length of ribbon
Two pairs 3,75mm knitting needles.

MEASUREMENTS:
Oliver measures 32cm(12½ins) when
sitting.

TENSION:
SAVE TIME, TAKE TIME, CHECK TENSION.
22sts and 30 rows = 10cm(4ins) over
stocking stitch using 3,75mm needles.

Body

Begin at bottom
Using the appropriate needles and A,
cast on 16sts.
1st row: K.
2nd row: SHAPE BODY: P, inc into
first 4sts, p2sts, inc into next 4sts,
p2sts, inc into last 4sts = 28sts.
3rd row: K, inc into first 2sts, k10sts,
inc into next 4sts, k10sts, inc into last
2sts = 36sts.
4th row: P, inc into first 2sts, p14sts,
inc into next 4sts, p14sts, inc into last
2sts = 44sts.
5th row: K, inc into first st, k20sts, inc
into next 2sts, k20sts, inc into last st =
48sts.
6th row: P, inc into first st, p22sts, inc
into next 2sts, p22sts, inc into last st =
52sts.
7th row: K, inc 1 st at each end of row
= 54sts.
8th row: P26sts, inc into next 2sts,
p26sts = 56sts.
9th row: K, inc 1 st at each end of row
= 58sts.
10th row: P28sts, inc into next 2sts,
p28sts = 60sts.
11th row: K, inc 1 st at each end of
row = 62sts.
12th row: P30sts, inc into next 2sts,
p30sts = 64sts.
13th to 15th row: Inc 1 st at each end
of next and foll alt row = 68sts.
16th row: P.
17th row: K33sts, inc into next 2sts,
k33sts = 70sts.
18th to 20th row: Work in st st.

21st row: K, inc 1 st at each end of
row = 72sts.
22nd to 30th row: Work in st st.
31st row: K, dec 1 st (= work 2tog) at
each end of row = 70sts.
32nd to 34th row: Work in st st.
35th row: K, dec 1 st at each end of
row = 68sts.
36th row: P32sts, (p2tog) twice,
p32sts = 66sts.
37th to 41st row: Work in st st.
42nd row: P31sts, (p2tog) twice,
p31sts = 64sts.
43rd to 47th row: Work in st st.
48th row: P30sts, (p2tog) twice,
p30sts = 62sts.
49th to 51st row: Work in st st.
52nd row: P29sts, (p2tog) twice,
p29sts = 60sts.
53rd to 55th row: Work in st st.
56th row: P28sts, (p2tog) twice,
p28sts = 58sts.
57th row: K.
58th row: P27sts, (p2tog) twice,
p27sts = 56sts.
59th row: K.
60th row: P2tog, p24sts, (p2tog)
twice, p24sts, p2tog = 52sts.
61st to 63rd row: Work in st st.
64th row: P2tog, p22sts, (p2tog)
twice, p22sts, p2tog = 48sts.
65th row: K.
66th row: P22sts, (p2tog) twice,
p22sts = 46sts.
67th row: K.
68th row: P21sts, (p2tog) twice,
p21sts = 44sts.
69th and 70th row: Dec 1 st at each
end of next and foll row = 40sts.
71st row: K.
72nd row: P, dec 1 st at each end of
row = 38sts.
73rd row: K13sts, (k2tog) 6 times,
k13sts = 32sts.
74th row: P2tog, p2sts, (p2tog) 12
times, p2sts, p2tog = 18sts.
75th row: (K3tog) 6 times = 6sts.
76th row: P.
77th row: (K2tog) 3 times = 3sts.
78th row: P3tog, fasten off.

Head

Begin at neck edge
Using the appropriate needles and A,
cast on 40sts.
1st row: K.
2nd row: SHAPE HEAD: P17sts, inc
into next st, p4sts, inc into next st,
p17sts = 42sts.
3rd and 4th row: Work in st st.

5th row: K18sts, inc into next 2sts,
k2sts, inc into next 2sts, k18sts =
46sts.
6th to 8th row: Inc 1 st at each end of
next and foll alt row = 50sts.
9th row: K21sts, inc into next 2sts,
k4sts, inc into next 2sts, k21sts =
54sts.
10th to 12th row: Inc 1 st at each end
of every row = 60sts.
13th row: K, inc into first st, k25sts,
inc into next st, k6sts, inc into next st,
k25sts, inc into last st = 64sts.
14th row: P, inc into first st, p25sts,
inc into next st, p10sts, inc into next st,
p25sts, inc into last st = 68sts.
15th and 16th row: Inc 1 st at each
end of next and foll row = 72sts.
17th row: K, inc into first 2sts, k29sts,
inc into next st, k8sts, inc into next st,
k29sts, inc into last 2sts = 78sts.
18th to 20th row: Inc 2sts at each end
of every row = 90sts.
21st row: K39sts, inc into next st,
k10sts, inc into next st, k39sts = 92sts.
22nd to 26th row: Work in st st.
27th row: K39sts, inc into next st,
k12sts, inc into next st, k39sts = 94sts.
28th and 29th row: Work in st st.
30th row: P37sts, p2tog, p16sts,
p2tog, p37sts = 92sts.
31st and 32nd row: Work in st st.
33rd row: K36sts, k2tog, inc into next
st, k14sts, inc into next st, k2tog,
k36sts = 92sts.
34th row: P.
35th row: Cast off 15sts, k to end =
77sts.
36th row: Cast off 15sts, p19sts,
p2tog, p18sts, p2tog, p20sts = 60sts.
37th row: (K2tog) twice, k52sts,
(k2tog) twice = 56sts.
38th row: P2tog, p15sts, p2tog,
p18sts, p2tog, p15sts, p2tog = 52sts.
39th row: K, dec 1 st (= work 2tog) at
each end of row = 50sts.
40th row: P2tog, p12sts, p2tog,
p18sts, p2tog, p12sts, p2tog = 46sts.
41st row: K2tog, k10sts, k2tog,
k18sts, k2tog, k10sts, k2tog = 42sts.
42nd row: P2tog, p8sts, p2tog,
p18sts, p2tog, p8sts, p2tog = 38sts.
43rd row: (K2tog) 3 times, k2sts,
k2tog, k18sts, k2tog, k2sts, (k2tog) 3
times = 30sts.
44th and 45th row: Cast off 6sts at
beg of each row = 18sts.
46th to 51st row: Work in st st.
52nd row: P, dec 1 st (= work 2tog) at
each end of row = 16sts.
53rd to 55th row: Work in st st.

56th row: P, dec 1 st at each end of row = 14sts.
57th row: K.
58th to 60th row: Dec 1 st at each end of next and foll alt row = 10sts.
61st to 63rd row: Work in st st.
64th row: P, dec 1 st at each end of row = 8sts.
65th to 81st row: Work in st st.
82nd row: P, dec 1 st at each end of row = 6sts.
83rd to 85th row: Work in st st.
86th row: P, dec 1 st at each end of row = 4sts.
87th row: K.
Cast off all sts.

Ears

Make 2 pieces in A and 2 pieces in B
Using the appropriate needles and A or B, cast on 16sts.
1st to 5th row: Work in st st.
6th row: P, dec 1 st (= work 2tog) at each end of row = 14sts.
7th to 9th row: Work in st st.
10th to 14th row: Dec 1 st at each end of next and foll alt rows = 8sts.
15th row: K, dec 1 st at each end of row = 6sts.
Cast off.

Legs

Both Alike

Begin at foot: Using the appropriate needles and A, cast on 58sts.
1st to 5th row: Work in st st.
6th row: SHAPE FOOT: P, dec 1 st (= work 2tog) at each end of row = 56sts.
7th row: K.
8th row: P26sts, (p2tog) twice, p26sts = 54sts.

9th to 11th row: Work in st st.
12th row: P25sts, (p2tog) twice, p25sts = 52sts.
13th row: K.
14th row: P2tog, p22sts, (p2tog) twice, p22sts, p2tog = 48sts.
15th row: K.
16th row: P22sts, (p2tog) twice, p22sts = 46sts.
17th row: K21sts, (k2tog) twice, k21sts = 44sts.
18th row: P20sts, (p2tog) twice, p20sts = 42sts.
19th row: K19sts, (k2tog) twice, k19sts = 40sts.
20th row: P.
Break off yarn and leave these sts on a needle.
LEFT SIDE: Using the appropriate needles and A, cast on 4sts.
1st and 2nd row: Work in st st.
3rd and 4th row: Inc 1 st at each end of next and foll row = 8sts.
5th row: K, inc into first st, k to last 2sts, inc into last 2sts = 11sts.
6th and 7th row: Inc 1 st at each end of next and foll row = 15sts.
8th row: P.
9th to 11th row: Work to last st, inc into last st on every row = 18sts.
12th row: P.
13th row: K, inc into first st, k to end = 19sts.
14th and 15th row: Work in st st.
16th row: P, inc 1 st at each end of row = 21sts.
17th and 18th row: Work in st st.
Break off yarn and leave these sts on a needle.
RIGHT SIDE: Using the appropriate needles and A, cast on 4sts.
1st and 2nd row: Work in st st.
3rd and 4th row: Inc 1 st at each end of next and foll row = 8sts.
5th row: K, inc into first 2sts, k to last

st, inc into last st = 11sts.
6th and 7th row: Inc 1 st at each end of next and foll row = 15sts.
8th row: P.
9th to 11th row: Inc 1 st at beg of every row = 18sts.
12th row: P.
13th row: K to last st, inc into last st = 19sts.
14th and 15th row: Work in st st.
16th row: P, inc 1 st at each end of row = 21sts.
17th and 18th row: Work in st st.
19th row: K to last st, inc into last st, now work across foot section as folls: K16sts, (k2tog) 4 times, k16sts, now work across left side as follows: Inc into first st, k to end of row = 80sts.
20th row: P36sts, (p2tog) 4 times, p36sts = 76sts.
21st row: K, inc into first st, k31sts, (k2tog) 6 times, k31sts, inc into last st = 72sts.
22nd row: P.
23rd row: K34sts, (k2tog) twice, k34sts = 70sts.
24th row: P.
25th row: K, dec 1 st at each end of row = 68sts.
26th and 27th row: Work in st st.
28th to 30th row: Dec 1 st at each end of next and foll alt row = 64sts.
31st row: K30sts, (k2tog) twice, k30sts = 62sts.
32nd to 34th row: Dec 1 st at each end of next and foll alt row = 58sts.
35th row: K27sts, (k2tog) twice, k27sts = 56sts.
36th and 37th row: Dec 1 st at each end of next and foll row = 52sts.
38th row: P24sts, (p2tog) twice, p24sts = 50sts.
39th and 40th row: Dec 1 st at each end of next and foll row = 46sts.
41st row: K21sts, (k2tog) twice, k21sts = 44sts.
42nd row: P, dec 1 st at each end of row = 42sts.
43rd row: K2tog, k17sts, (k2tog) twice, k17sts, k2tog = 38sts.
44th row: (P2tog) twice, p13sts, (p2tog) twice, p13sts, (p2tog) twice = 32sts.
45th row: K2tog, k12sts, (k2tog) twice, k12sts, k2tog = 28sts.
46th row: P2tog, p8sts, (p2tog) 4 times, p8sts, p2tog = 22sts.
Cast off.

Soles

Both Alike
Using the appropriate needles and B, cast on 4sts.
1st row: K.
2nd to 5th row: Inc 1 st at each end of every row = 12sts.

6th row: P.

7th row: K, inc 1 st at each end of row = 14sts.

8th to 31st row: Work in st st.

32nd to 34th row: Dec 1 st at each end of next and foll alt row = 10sts.

35th to 37th row: Dec 1 st at each end of every row = 4sts.

38th row: P.
Cast off.

Arms

Both Alike
Using the appropriate needles and A, cast on 8sts.

1st row: K.

2nd row: **SHAPE ARM:** *P, inc into first 2sts, p1*, rep from * to * once more, inc into last 2sts = 14sts.

3rd row: K, inc into first st, k5sts, inc into next 2sts, k5sts, inc into last st = 18sts.

4th row: P, inc into first st, p7sts, inc into next 2sts, p7sts, inc into last st = 22sts.

5th row: K, inc 1 st at each end of row = 24sts.

6th row: P11sts, inc into next 2sts, p11sts = 26sts.

7th and 8th row: Inc 1 st at each end of next and foll row = 30sts.

9th row: K.

10th to 12th row: Inc 1 st at each end of next and foll alt row = 34sts.

13th row: K.

14th row: P, inc 1 st at each end of row = 36sts.

15th row: K, inc into first st, k15sts, (k2tog) twice, k15sts, inc into last st = 36sts.

16th row: P.

17th row: K16sts, (k2tog) twice, k16sts = 34sts.

18th row: P.

19th row: K, inc 1 st at each end of row = 36sts.

20th row: P16sts, (p2tog) twice, p16sts = 34sts.

21st row: K.

22nd row: P, inc into first st, p14sts, (p2tog) twice, p14sts, inc into last st = 34sts.

23rd row: K15sts, (k2tog) twice, k15sts = 32sts.

24th row: P14sts, (p2tog) twice, p14sts = 30sts.

25th row: K, inc 1 st at each end of row = 32sts.

26th row: P14sts, (p2tog) twice, p14sts = 30sts.

27th to 29th row: Work in st st.

30th row: P, inc into first st, p12sts, (p2tog) twice, p12sts, inc into last st = 30sts.

31st to 37th row: Work in st st.

38th row: P, inc 1 st at each end of row = 32sts.

39th row: K15sts, inc into next 2sts, k15sts = 34sts.

40th to 48th row: Work in st st.

49th row: K16sts, inc into next 2sts, k16sts = 36sts.

50th to 57th row: Work in st st.

58th row: P2tog, p14sts, (p2tog) twice, p14sts, p2tog = 32sts.

59th to 61st row: Work in st st.

62nd row: P2tog, p12sts, (p2tog) twice, p12sts, p2tog = 28sts.

63rd row: K.

64th row: P2tog, p10sts, (p2tog) twice, p10sts, p2tog = 24sts.

65th row: K2tog, k8sts, (k2tog) twice, k8sts, k2tog = 20sts.

66th row: P2tog, p6sts, (p2tog) twice, p6sts, p2tog = 16sts.

67th row: K2tog to end = 8sts.

68th row: P2tog to end = 4sts.

69th row: (K2tog) twice = 2sts.

70th row: P2tog, fasten off.

To Make Up:

Sew all pieces using back stitch (see general instructions). **BODY:** With right sides to inside sew back seam closed leaving an opening for stuffing. Stuff firmly and ladder stitch (see general instructions) the gap closed. **HEAD:** With right sides to inside sew side seams of head gusset (see diagram 1 on page 12), then muzzle seam (see diagram 2), leaving neck (cast on edge) open. If nose and eyes need to be attached before stuffing, do so now (see general instructions). Stuff head and nose firmly. Using a new thread, run a gathering stitch around neck (cast on edge) at head and pull in tightly. Fasten off. Pin head to body ensuring nose seam and centre front of body are in line. Sew head firmly to body by pressing head down onto the body and sewing, making sure that the head remains straight on the body. The firmer you press the head onto the body, the more stable the head will be. **EARS:** With right sides to inside sew curved edge leaving cast on edge open. Stuff ears very lightly and sew closed using ladder stitch. Pin to head in desired position. Sew firmly to head ensuring neat edges. **LEGS:** Fold in half with right sides to inside, and sew seams leaving an opening for stuffing. Sew sole (RS to inside) into position at base of foot. Turn right side out and stuff legs and feet firmly. Close opening. Pin legs to body in desired position (see picture), ensuring that they are equally placed on either side of body. Sew legs firmly to body taking care to sew a fairly large section of leg to the body to ensure firm posture. **ARMS:** Fold in half with right sides to inside, and sew seams leaving an opening for stuffing. Turn right side out and stuff firmly. Close opening. Pin arms to body as close to the head as possible ensuring that they are of equal distance on either side of body. Sew firmly to body (arms will drop slightly away from head when complete). Embroider mouth (see general instructions). Tie ribbon around neck.

Professor Rusty

MATERIALS
Professor Rusty
RUSTICA DOUBLE KNIT
150g colour of your choice
One pair 12mm amber glass eyes
One 30mm black felt nose
Pipe
Pair of Spectacles
Briefcase
Fob watch
Oddments of dark brown yarn for embroidery
Polyester stuffing
One pair 3mm knitting needles
Waistcoat and Bow Tie
FAMILY KNIT DK
Waistcoat: 50g Peat Brown
3 buttons
Bow Tie: Oddments of Red
One pair 4mm knitting needles.

MEASUREMENTS
Professor Rusty measures 30cm(11¾ins) sitting and 46cm(18ins) standing.
Waistcoat:
Actual all round measurement: 38cm(15ins)
Length to back neck: 12cm(4¾ins)

TENSION:
SAVE TIME, TAKE TIME, CHECK TENSION.
26sts and 36 rows = 10cm(4ins) over stocking stitch using 3mm needles.
22sts and 30 rows = 10cm(4ins) over stocking stitch using 4mm needles.

Basic Bear

Work as for bear pattern OSCAR but using 3mm needles throughout.

Waistcoat

Back

Using 4mm needles cast on 41sts.
Beg with a p row work 9 rows st st. (first row = WS).
SHAPE ARMHOLES: Cast off 4sts at beg of next 2 rows = 33sts.
Dec 1 st (= work 2tog) at each end of next and every foll alt row 4 times in all = 25sts
St st 17 rows.
Next row; SHAPE BACK NECK: K9, cast off centre 7sts and cont on rem sts

for left side of work. **LEFT SIDE:** Dec 1 st at neck edge in every row 3 times, cast off rem 6sts. **RIGHT SIDE:** WSF, rejoin yarn to rem 9sts and dec 1 st at neck edge in every row 3 times, then cast off rem 6sts.

Left Front

Using 4mm needles cast on 2sts. P one row (1st row = WS). Cont in st st inc 1 st at each end of every row until there are 16sts.
Work one row**.
Cast on 4sts at beg of next row, then 2sts at beg of foll row = 22sts.
St st 9 rows.
SHAPE ARMHOLE: Cast off 4sts at beg of next row = 18sts.
Dec 1 st at armhole edge on every alt row 4 times = 14sts.
Work one row.
SHAPE NECK: Dec 1 st at end (= front edge) of next and foll alt row 8 times = 6sts.
St st 3 rows, then cast off.

Right Front

Work as for left front to **.
Cast on 2sts at beg of next row and 4sts at beg of foll row = 22sts.
St st 2 rows.
Next row, buttonhole row: K2, yfd, k2tog, k to end.
St st 5 rows.
Next row: Work buttonhole as before.

SHAPE ARMHOLE: Cast off 4sts at beg of next row = 18sts.
Dec 1st at armhole edge on next and foll alt row = 16sts
Next row: Work buttonhole as before.
Dec 1 st at armhole edge on next and foll alt row = 14sts.
St st 2 rows.
SHAPE NECK: Dec 1 st at beg (= front edge) of next and foll alt row 8 times = 6sts.
St st 3 rows, then cast off.

To Make Up

Block pieces to measurement, cover with a damp cloth and allow to dry. Sew shoulder and side seams. Sew on buttons.

Bow Tie

Using 4mm needles and red, cast on 28sts and work 2 rows g st (see general instructions). Beg with a k row, work in st st for 4 rows. P one row, then cast off kw.

To Make Up

Oversew row ends together and turn right side out. Place oversewn seam at centre back of the bow. Tie a long length of yarn around centre of oversewn seam, wind tightly around centre of bow several times and knot firmly. Use remaining length of yarn to tie bow around neck.

PROFESSOR RUSTY

Ming

MATERIALS
ALASKA
150g each White A and Black B.
One pair 12mm light blue glass eyes
One 32mm black felt nose
Oddments of black yarn for
embroidery
Polyester stuffing
One pair 4,5mm knitting needles

MEASUREMENTS
Ming measures 40cm(15¾ins) sitting
and 62cm(24½ins) standing.

TENSION:
SAVE TIME, TAKE TIME, CHECK TENSION.
15sts and 23 rows = 10cm(4ins) over
stocking stitch using 4,5mm needles.

Basic Bear

Work as for bear pattern OSCAR but
using 4,5mm needles throughout.

Head and Body

Worked in A.

Arms, Legs, Soles and Ears

Worked in B.

Eye Patches

Using 4,5mm needles and B, cast on
5sts.
1st row: K.
2nd row: Inc into first st, k to last st, inc
into last st.
Rep last 2 rows once more = 9sts.
5th to 7th row: K.
8th row: K2tog, k to last 2sts, k2tog.
9th row: K.
Rep last 2 rows once more = 5sts.
Cast off.

Tail

Using 4,5mm needles and B, cast on
16sts.
1st row: P.
2nd row: K3sts, inc into next 4sts,
k2sts, inc into next 4sts, k3sts = 24sts.
3rd to 5th row: Work in st st.
6th row: K3sts, (k2tog) 4 times, k2sts,
(k2tog) 4 times, k3sts = 16sts.
7th row: P.
8th row: K1 st, (k2tog) 7 times, k1 st =
9sts.
Pull thread tightly through sts and
fasten off.
Sew row ends together and turn right
side out.

To Make Up

Work as for Oscar. Sew eye patches
onto face (see picture) and attach
eyes. Stuff tail and sew open end of
tail to back of bear (see picture).

MING

Candy and Cody

MATERIALS

CAPRI

CODY: 200g Hessian A and 50g Rich Cream B.

CANDY: 200g Rich Cream A and 50g Hessian B.

For Candy: One pair 14mm amethyst eyes and one pair brown eyelids.
Lace collar.
Straw basket and flowers.

For Cody: One pair 14mm brown glass eyes and one pair black eyelids.

Both bears: One each brown 25mm oval flocked nose.
Oddments of brown yarn for embroidery.
Polyester stuffing.
One pair 3mm knitting needles.

PULLOVER

100g Family Knit DK.
3 buttons.
One pair each 3,25mm and 4mm knitting needles.
One 3mm crochet hook.
One cable needle.
Stitch holders.

MEASUREMENTS:

Candy and Cody measure 30cm(11¾ins) sitting and 48cm(19ins) standing.

Pullover:
Actual all round measurement: 40cm(15¾ins).
Length to shoulder: 15cm(6ins).
Sleeve length: 14cm(5½ins).

TENSION:

SAVE TIME, TAKE TIME, CHECK TENSION.
24sts and 34 rows = 10cm(4ins) over stocking stitch using 3mm needles and Capri.
22sts and 30 rows = 10cm(4ins) over stocking stitch using 4mm needles and Family Knit DK.

Basic Bear

Work as for bear pattern OSCAR but using 3mm needles throughout.

Ears

For both bears
Work 2 pieces in A and 2 pieces in B (see picture).

Soles

Work using B (see picture).

Pullover

Back

Using 3,25mm needles cast on 37sts and work in rib patt (see general instructions) for 7 rows. **Next row, inc row:** Rib one row on WS inc 12sts evenly across row = 49sts. Change to 4mm needles and cont in patt as folls: **1st row:** RSF, (p1, k1) 3 times, p3, k2, C4F, p3, k1, (p1, k1) 6 times, p3, k2, C4F, p3, (k1, p1) 3 times. **2nd row:** (K1, p1) 3 times, k3, p6, k3, p1, (k1, p1) 6 times, k3, p6, k3, (p1, k1) 3 times. **3rd row:** (K1, p1) 3 times, k1, p2, C4B, k2, p2, k1, (p1, k1) 7 times, p2, C4B, k2, p2, k1, (p1, k1) 3 times. **4th row:** (P1, k1) 3 times, p1, k2, p6, k2, p1, (k1, p1) 7 times, k2, p6, k2, p1, (k1, p1) 3 times. These 4 rows form the patt. Cont straight in patt and when back measures 15cm(6ins) from beg ending with a WSR, **SHAPE SHOULDERS:** Keeping patt correct cast off 16sts at beg of next 2 rows. Sl rem 17sts onto a holder.

Front

Work as for back until front is 9 rows shorter than back to shoulder thus ending with a RSR, **SHAPE NECK:** Patt 20sts, turn and complete this side first. *Dec 1 st at neck edge on next 3 rows, then foll alt row once = 16sts. Work 4 rows straight (1 row less for other side), thus ending at side edge. Cast off in patt. Sl next 9sts at centre onto a safety pin. WSF, rejoin yarn to remaining 20sts and patt to end. Work as for first side from * to end.

Sleeves

Both Alike
Using 3,25mm needles cast on 27sts and work 5 rows in rib patt. **Next row, inc row:** Rib one row on WS inc 7sts evenly across row = 34sts. Change to 4mm needles and cont in patt as folls: **1st row:** RSF, (p1, k1) 6 times, p2, k2, C4F, p2, (k1, p1) 6 times. **2nd row:** (K1, p1) 6 times, k2, p6, k2, (p1, k1) 6 times. **3rd row:** (K1, p1) 5 times, k1, p3, C4B, k2, p3, k1, (p1, k1) 5 times. **4th row:** (P1, k1) 5 times, p1, k3, p6, k3, p1, (k1, p1) 5 times. These 4 rows form the patt. Keeping patt correct and bringing extra sts into double moss st, inc 1 st at each end of next and every foll 4th row until there are 46sts. Work 11 rows straight, thus ending with a WSR. Cast off in patt.

To Make Up

Block pieces to measurement, cover with a damp cloth and allow to dry. Sew right shoulder seam. **NECKBAND:** RSF, using 3,25mm needles pick up and k8sts down left front slope, k across sts on safety pin at centre front, pick up and k8sts up right front slope, then k across sts on holder at back neck dec 1 st (= work 2tog) at centre = 41sts. Work 4 rows in rib patt, then cast off loosely RW. **SHOULDER EDGING:** RSF, using 3,25mm needles beg at top of neckband, pick up and k15sts along back shoulder, then cast off kw. Beg at side edge, pick up and k sts in the same way along front shoulder. Lay front shoulder edging over back shoulder edging and pin together at side edge. Fold sleeves in half lengthways and placing centre of cast off edge to shoulder seam, sew sleeves in position. Sew side and sleeve seams. Using a 3mm crochet hook work one row dc around shoulder opening, working 3 buttonholes evenly on back shoulder. Sew on buttons.

Blue

MATERIALS:

TRUE BLUE DK
200g Light Denim for bear
50g Navy for dungarees
2 small buttons
Oddments of red yarn for heart insert
Oddments of black yarn for embroidery
One pair 11mm black glass eyes
One 21mm black plastic nose
Denim school satchel
Polyester stuffing
One pair each 2,75mm and 3mm knitting needles

MEASUREMENTS:

Blue measures 27cm(10½ins) sitting and 44cm(17½ins) standing.

TENSION:

SAVE TIME, TAKE TIME, CHECK TENSION
26sts and 36 rows = 10cm(4ins) over stocking stitch using 3mm needles.

Basic Bear

Work as for bear pattern OSCAR but using 3mm needles throughout.

Dungarees

Beg at lower edge of right leg.
Using 3mm needles cast on 70sts and work 4 rows g st, then cont in st st until work measures 10cm(4ins) from beg ending with a WSR.
SHAPE CROTCH: Cast off 2sts at beg of next 2 rows and 1 st at beg of next 4 rows.
**Cut yarn and leave rem 62sts on a spare needle.
Work left leg in same way to **.
Next row: K sts of left leg then k sts of right leg.
Cont in st st on 124sts as folls:
Next row: WSF, p. **Next row:** K2sts, inc into next st, k2sts, inc into next st, k to last 6sts, inc into next st, k2sts, inc into next st, k2sts. **Next row:** P. Rep last 2 rows 3 times more = 140sts. St st 2 rows. **Next row:** K2sts, k2tog, k2sts, k2tog, k to last 8sts, k2tog, k2sts, k2tog, k2sts. **Next row:** P. Rep last 2 rows 3 times more = 124sts. Cont straight until work measures 18cm(7ins) from beg ending with a RSR. **Next row, dec row:** P3tog, p2sts, (p2tog, p2sts) 29 times, p3tog =

91sts. Change to 2,75mm needles and work in rib patt (see general instructions) for 2 rows. **Next row, buttonhole row:** Rib 10sts, cast off 2sts, rib to last 12sts, cast off 2sts, rib to end. **Next row:** Rib, casting on 2sts over each buttonhole. Work 2 more rows in rib. **Next row:** Cast off 30sts RW, rib until there are 6sts on right needle, place these sts on a safety pin for shoulder strap, k next 19sts (= bib), work next 6sts in rib and place onto another safety pin, then cast off rem 30sts RW, fasten off. **BIB FRONT:** WSF, using 3mm needles rejoin yarn to 19sts of bib and work in st st for 6cm ending with a WSR. Now using 2,75mm needles, work 4 rows in rib patt, then cast off loosely RW. **SHOULDER STRAPS:** WSF, using 2,75mm needles rejoin yarn to outer edge of right shoulder strap, (k1, p1) twice, k1 st, then inc in next st = 7sts.
1st row: K2sts, (p1, k1) twice, k1 st.
2nd row: (K1, p1) 3 times, k1 st. Rep these 2 rows until strap measures 21cm(8¼ins) then cast off RW. WSF,

rejoin yarn to inner edge of left shoulder strap, inc in first st, (k1, p1) twice, k1 = 7sts. Complete as for right shoulder strap.

To Make Up

Sew short crotch seam at centre front and entire centre back seam. Sew inner leg seams. Sew inner edge of shoulder straps to sides of bib front and sew a button to end of each strap. Swiss darn (see general instructions) heart in centre of bib (see chart and picture).

BLUE

Henry

MATERIALS:
LUSSURIA and VELLUTO
250g White Lussuria
50g White Velluto
One pair 18mm black glass eyes
One 25mm black plastic nose
Oddments of black yarn for embroidery
Length of ribbon
Polyester stuffing
One pair each 3,75mm and 4mm knitting needles.

MEASUREMENTS:
Henry measures 30cm(11¾ins) sitting and 45cm(17¾ins) standing.

TENSION:
SAVE TIME, TAKE TIME, CHECK TENSION.
21sts and 30 rows = 10cm(4ins) over stocking stitch using 3,75mm needles and Lussuria.
22sts and 30 rows = 10cm(4ins) over stocking stitch using 3,75mm needles and Velluto.

Basic Bear

Body and arms worked as for bear pattern OSCAR. Ears: Work 2 pieces in Lussuria and 2 pieces in Velluto.

Head

Begin at neck edge
Using 3,75mm needles and Lussuria, cast on 40sts.
1st row: K.
2nd row: SHAPE HEAD: P17sts, inc into next st, p4sts, inc into next st, p17sts = 42sts.
3rd and 4th row: Work in st st.
5th row: K18sts, inc into next 2sts, k2sts, inc into next 2sts, k18sts = 46sts.
6th row: P, inc 1 st at each end of row = 48sts.
7th row: K.
8th row: P, inc 1 st at each end of row = 50sts.
9th row: K21sts, inc into next 2sts, k4sts, inc into next 2sts, k21sts = 54sts.
10th to 12th row: Inc 1 st at each end of every row = 60sts.
13th row: K, inc into first st, k25sts, inc into next st, k6sts, inc into next st, k25sts, inc into last st = 64sts.
14th row: Using Velluto, inc into first st, using Lussuria, p25sts, inc into next st, p10sts, inc into next st, p25sts, using Velluto, inc into last st = 68sts.
15th row: Using Velluto, inc into first st, k1 st, using Lussuria, k to last 2sts, using Velluto, k1 st, inc into last st = 70sts.
16th row: Using Velluto inc into first st, p2sts, using Lussuria, p to last 3sts, using Velluto, p2sts, inc into last st = 72sts.
17th row: Using Velluto, inc into first 2sts, k2sts, using Lussuria, k27sts, inc into next st, k8sts, inc into next st, k27sts, using Velluto, k2sts, inc into last 2sts = 78sts.
18th row: Using Velluto, inc into first 2sts, p4sts, using Lussuria, p66sts, using Velluto, p4sts, inc into last 2sts = 82sts.
19th row: Using Velluto, inc into first 2sts, k7sts, using Lussuria, k64sts, using Velluto, k7sts, inc into last 2sts = 86sts.
20th row: Using Velluto, inc into first 2sts, p9sts, using Lussuria, p64sts, using Velluto, p9sts, then inc into last 2sts = 90sts.
21st row: Using Velluto, k14sts, using Lussuria, k25sts, inc into next st, k10sts, inc into next st, k25sts, using Velluto, k14sts = 92sts.
22nd to 26th row: Work in st st using Velluto and Lussuria as they appear.
NOTE: Keeping yarns as they appear continue as folls:-
27th row: K39sts, inc into next st, k12sts, inc into next st, k39sts = 94sts.
28th and 29th row: Work in st st.
30th row: P37sts, p2tog, p16sts, p2tog, p37sts = 92sts.
31st and 32nd row: Work in st st.
33rd row: K36sts, k2tog, inc into next st, k14sts, inc into next st, k2tog, k36sts = 92sts.
34th row: P.
35th row: Cast off 15sts at beg of row, k to end = 77sts.
36th row: Cast off 15sts, p19sts, p2tog, p18sts, p2tog, p20sts = 60sts.
37th row: (K2tog) twice, k52sts, (k2tog) twice = 56sts.
38th row: P2tog, p15sts, p2tog, p18sts, p2tog, p15sts, p2tog = 52sts.
39th row: K, dec 1 st (= work 2tog) at each end of row = 50sts.
40th row: P2tog, p12sts, p2tog, p18sts, p2tog, p12sts, p2tog = 46sts.
41st row: K2tog, k10sts, k2tog, k18sts, k2tog, k10sts, k2tog = 42sts.
42nd row: P2tog, p8sts, p2tog, p18sts, p2tog, p8sts, p2tog = 38sts.
43rd row: (K2tog) 3 times, k2sts, k2tog, k18sts, k2tog, k2sts, (k2tog) 3 times = 30sts.
44th and 45th row: Cast off 6sts at beg of each row = 18sts.
46th to 51st row: Work in st st.
52nd row: P, dec 1 st at each end of row = 16sts.
53rd to 55th row: Work in st st.
56th row: P, dec 1 st at each end of row = 14sts.
57th row: K.
58th to 60th row: Dec 1 st at each

end of next and foll alt row = 10sts.

61st to 63rd row: Work in st st.

64th row: P, dec 1 st at each end of row = 8sts.

65th to 68th row: Work in st st. Change to Velluto for muzzle.

69th to 81st row: Work in st st.

82nd row: P, dec 1 st at each end of row = 6sts.

83rd to 85th row: Work in st st.

86th row: P, dec 1 st at each end of row = 4sts.

87th row: K.

Cast off all sts.

Legs

Both Alike

Using 4mm needles and Lussuria, cast on 68sts.

1st to 5th row: Work in st st.

6th row: SHAPE FOOT: P32sts, (p2tog) twice, p32sts = 66sts.

7th row: K31sts, (k2tog) twice, k31sts = 64sts.

8th row: P30sts, (p2tog) twice, p30sts = 62sts.

9th row: K29sts, (k2tog) twice, k29sts = 60sts.

10th row: P28sts, (p2tog) twice, p28sts = 58sts.

11th row: K27sts, (k2tog) twice, k27sts = 56sts.

12th row: P26sts, (p2tog) twice, p26sts = 54sts.

13th row: K25sts, (k2tog) twice, k25sts = 52sts.

14th row: P22sts, (p2tog) 4 times, p22sts = 48sts.

15th row: K22sts, (k2tog) twice, k22sts = 46sts.

16th row: P17sts, (p2tog) 6 times, p17sts = 40sts.

17th row: K18sts, (k2tog) twice, k18sts = 38sts.

18th row: P15sts, (p2tog) 4 times, p15sts = 34sts.

19th row: K15sts, (k2tog) twice, k15sts = 32sts.

20th row: P14sts, (p2tog) twice, p14sts = 30sts. Change to 3,75mm needles and complete as for basic pattern OSCAR'S legs from *** to end.

Soles

Both Alike

Using 3,75mm needles and Velluto, cast on 2sts.

1st row: K.

2nd row: Cast on 2sts, p to end of row = 4sts.

3rd row: Cast on 2sts, k to end of row = 6sts.

4th row: P, inc 1 st at each end of row = 8sts.

5th row: K.

6th row: P, inc 1 st at each end of row = 10sts.

7th row: K.

8th row: P, inc 1 st at each end of row = 12sts.

9th row: K.

10th row: P, inc 1 st at each end of row = 14sts.

11th to 44th row: Work in st st.

45th row: K2tog, k to last 2sts, k2tog = 12sts.

46th row: P.

47th row: K2tog, k to last 2sts, k2tog = 10sts.

48th row: P.

49th row: K2tog, k to last 2sts, k2tog = 8sts.

50th row: P.

51st row: K2tog, k to last 2sts, k2tog = 6sts.

52nd row: P.

53rd row: (K2tog) twice, k to end = 4sts.

54th row: (P2tog) twice = 2sts.

55th row: K2tog, fasten off.

To Make Up

Work as for bear pattern OSCAR, but on completion of feet, using black yarn embroider 3 long straight sts on base of each sole for claws (see picture). Tie ribbon around neck.

Snowy

MATERIALS
ALASKA
350g White
One pair 20mm black glass eyes.
One 40mm black felt nose trimmed to shape (see picture).
Oddments of black yarn for embroidery.
Polyester stuffing.
One pair 4,5mm knitting needles.

MEASUREMENTS:
Snowy measures 64cm(25¼ins) lying down.

TENSION:
SAVE TIME, TAKE TIME, CHECK TENSION.
15sts and 23 rows = 10cm(4ins) over stocking stitch using 4,5mm needles.

Basic Bear

Work as for bear pattern OLIVER but using 4,5mm needles throughout.
Ears and Soles: Use white only.

Tail

Using 4,5mm needles cast on 16sts.
1st row: P.
2nd row: K3sts, inc into next 4sts, k2sts, inc into next 4sts, k3sts = 24sts.
3rd to 5th row: Work in st st.
6th row: K3sts, (k2tog) 4 times, k2sts, (k2tog) 4 times, k3sts = 16sts.
7th row: P.
8th row: K1 st, (k2tog) 7 times, k1 st = 9sts.
Pull thread tightly through sts and fasten off.
Sew row ends together and turn right side out.

To Make Up

As this bear is lying down, the centre back seam now becomes the centre front seam. Position arms and legs in place with body lying flat, sew firmly in place (see picture). Position head on body so that the chin rests on the paws, sew in place. It is important that a larger section of the head i.e. about a third of the way up the back of the head, is sewn to the body to achieve a firmer effect. Stuff tail and sew open end of tail into position (see picture).

SNOWY

Preston and Beasley

MATERIALS
BOTH BEARS
MOHAIR 2000
200g Light Grey A and 50g Charcoal B for each bear
One pair 12mm grey and 14mm black glass eyes for each bear
One 18mm black plastic nose for each bear
One Top Hat and Cane for each bear
One stiff white collar and bow tie for each bear
Oddments of black yarn for embroidery
Polyester stuffing
One pair 4mm knitting needles
WAISTCOAT FOR PRESTON
FAMILY KNIT DK
50g Black
3 buttons
One pair 4mm knitting needles.
EVENING JACKET FOR BEASLEY
FAMILY KNIT DK
100g Black
3 buttons
One pair 4mm knitting needles.

MEASUREMENTS:
Preston and Beasley measure 32cm(12½ins) sitting and 47cm(18½ins) standing.
Waistcoat:
Actual all round measurement: 46cm(18ins)
Length to back neck: 15cm(6ins)
Jacket:
Actual all round measurement: 44cm(17½ins)
Back length to tip of tails: 28cm(11ins)
Sleeve length: 16cm(6½ins)

TENSION:
SAVE TIME, TAKE TIME, CHECK TENSION.
18sts and 24 rows = 10cm(4ins) over stocking stitch using 4mm needles and Mohair.
22sts and 30 rows = 10cm(4ins) over stocking stitch using 4mm needles and Family Knit DK.

Basic Bear

Work as for bear pattern OSCAR but using 4mm needles throughout. Work soles in B. For ears, work 2 pieces in A and 2 pieces in B.

PALACE THEATRE

Presents

A Teddy Affair

Rage of the Grizzley

Forthcoming Attractions

The Bear Story

Presented by

Teddyville Studio

Forthcoming Attractions
Planet of the Bears

Presents
A Teddy Affair
Rage of the Grizzl...

Waistcoat

Back

Using 4mm needles cast on 41sts. Beg with a p row work 19 rows st st (1st row = WS). **SHAPE ARMHOLES:** Cast off 4sts at beg of next 2 rows = 33sts. Dec 1 st at each end of next and foll alt row 4 times in all = 25sts. St st 17 rows. **Next row; SHAPE BACK NECK:** K9sts, cast off centre 7sts and cont on rem sts for left side of work. **LEFT SIDE:** Dec 1 st (= work 2tog) at neck edge in every row 3 times, cast off rem 6sts. **RIGHT SIDE:** WSF, rejoin yarn to rem 9sts and dec 1 st at neck edge in every row 3 times, then cast off rem 6sts.

Left Front

Using 4mm needles cast on 2sts. P one row (= WS). Cont in st st inc 1 st at each end of every row until there are 16sts. Work one row**. Cast on 4sts at beg of next row, then 2sts at beg of foll row = 22sts. St st 15 rows. **SHAPE ARMHOLE:** Cast off 4sts at beg of next row = 18sts. Dec 1 st at armhole edge every alt row 4 times = 14sts. Work one row. **SHAPE NECK:** Dec 1 st at end (= front edge) of next and foll alt row 8 times = 6sts. St st 7 rows, then cast off.

Right Front

Work as for left front to **. Cast on 2sts at beg of next row and 4sts at beg of foll row = 22sts. St st 2 rows. **Next row, buttonhole row:** K2sts, yfd, k2tog, k to end. St st 9 rows. **Next row:** Work buttonhole as before. St st 9 rows. **Next row:** Work buttonhole as before. **AT THE SAME TIME** when work measures same as left front to armhole, **SHAPE ARMHOLE:** Cast off 4sts at armhole edge = 18sts. Dec 1st at armhole edge every alt row 4 times = 14sts. Work 2 rows. **SHAPE NECK:** Dec 1 st at beg (= front edge) of next and foll alt row 8 times = 6sts. St st 7 rows, then cast off.

To Make Up

Block pieces to measurement, cover with a damp cloth and allow to dry. Sew shoulder and side seams. Sew on buttons.

Jacket With Tails

Left Front

Using 4mm needles cast on 2sts. P one row (= WS). Cont in st st, inc 1 st at each end of every foll alt row until there are 16sts. Work one row**. Cast on 4sts at beg of next row, then 2sts at beg of foll row = 22sts. St st 25 rows. **SHAPE NECK:** Dec 1 st (= work 2tog) at beg (= front edge) of next and every foll alt row 10 times = 12sts. St st 6 rows, then cast off.

Right Front

Work as for left front to **. Cast on 2sts at beg of next row and 4sts at beg of foll row = 22sts. St st 2 rows. **Next row, buttonhole row:** K2sts, yfd, k2tog, k to end. St st 9 rows. **Next row:** Work buttonhole as before. St st 9 rows. Work buttonhole as before. Work one row. **SHAPE NECK:** Dec 1 st at beg (= front edge) of next and every foll alt row 10 times = 12sts. St st 7 rows, then cast off.

Right Back

Make 2
Cast on 2sts. P one row (= WS). **Next row:** K1, inc into next st. **Next row:** P. **Next row:** K to last 2sts, inc into next st, k1. **Next row:** P. Rep last 2 rows 18 times more = 22sts. Now cont straight in st st until side seam measures same as back to shoulder, then cast off all sts.

Left Back

Make 2
Work as for right back rev shapings.

Sleeves

Both Alike
Using 3,25mm needles cast on 41sts and work 4 rows in g st, inc 2sts evenly across last row = 43sts. Change to 4mm needles and cont in st st, inc 1 st at each end of every foll 4th row until there are 51sts. Cont straight until work measures 16cm from beg ending with a WSR, then cast off loosely.

To Make Up

Block pieces to measurement, cover with a damp cloth and allow to dry. **NOTE:** Back tail pieces are knitted double and sewn together to prevent curling. With right sides to inside, sew one left and one right back together leaving top end open. Rep with other two back pieces. Turn right side out and close top openings. Sew two backs together down centre back using ladder stitch, to beg of shaping. Sew front and back shoulder seams. Place markers 10cm down on either side of shoulder seams. Set in sleeves between markers. Sew up side and sleeve seams. Sew on buttons.

Monty

MATERIALS:
ALASKA AND CHUNKY
BEAR:
50g Taupe ALASKA and 200g Aran CHUNKY
One pair 18mm black glass eyes.
One 42mm black felt nose.
Oddments of black yarn for embroidery.
Polyester stuffing.
One pair 4,5mm knitting needles.
JUMPSUIT:
200g Taupe ALASKA
One 30mm zip.
One pair each 5mm and 5,5mm knitting needles.
Stitch holders.

MEASUREMENTS:
Monty measures 60cm(23½ins) standing and 40cm(15¾ins) sitting.
Jumpsuit:
Actual all round measurement: Chest: 60cm(23½ins)
Length to back neck: 45cm(17¾ins)
Sleeve seam: 15cm(6ins)

TENSION:
SAVE TIME, TAKE TIME, CHECK TENSION.
BEAR: 18sts and 26 rows = 10cm(4ins) over stocking stitch using 4,5mm needles and Chunky.
JUMPSUIT: 14sts and 19 rows = 10cm(4ins) over stocking stitch using 5,5mm needles and Alaska.

Basic Bear

Work as for bear pattern OSCAR but using 4,5mm needles throughout. Head and 2 pieces of Ears to be worked in Alaska. Body, Legs, Soles, Arms and 2 pieces of Ears to be worked in Chunky.

Jumpsuit

Feet

Both Alike
Using 5,5mm needles, cast on 52sts and work in st st for 5 rows. **SHAPE FOOT:** P24sts, (p2tog) twice, p24sts = 50sts. Work 3 rows st st. P23sts, (p2tog) twice, p23sts = 48sts. Work 3 rows st st. P20sts, (p2tog) 4 times, p20sts = 44sts. K20sts, (k2tog) twice,

k20sts = 42sts. P15sts, (p2tog) 6 times, p15sts = 36sts. K one row. P14sts, (p2tog) 4 times, p14sts = 32sts. K one row. P14sts, (p2tog) twice, p14sts = 30sts. Inc 7sts evenly across next and foll row = 44sts. Cast off all sts loosely.

Soles

Make two soles as for bear pattern OSCAR but using 5,5mm needles.

Back

FIRST LEG: Using 5,5mm needles cast on 24sts for lower edge of leg and cont straight in st st for 12cm(4¾ins) ending with a RSR**, cast off 1 st at beg of next row = 23sts. K one row. Cut yarn and leave these sts on a holder. **SECOND LEG:** Work as for first leg to **. P one row. Cast off 1 st at beg of next row. Now join the 2 legs by working across all sts as folls:- **Next row:** P23sts of second leg then p23sts of first leg = 46sts. **Next row:** K21sts, k2tog, SKPO, k21sts. **Next row:** P. **Next row:** K20sts, k2tog, SKPO, k20sts = 42sts***. Cont straight in st st and when work measures 30cm(11¾ins) from beg, ending with a WSR, **SHAPE ARMHOLES:** Cast off 2sts at beg of next 2 rows, then 1 st at beg of foll alt row 4 times in all = 34sts. Cont straight and when work measures 45cm(17¾ins) from beg, ending with a WSR, **SHAPE NECK:** K11sts and leave on a holder, cast off centre 12sts and cont on rem sts for left side of work. **LEFT SIDE:** Work one row. *Dec 1 st at beg (neck edge) of next 2 rows = 9sts. Cast off rem sts for shoulder. **RIGHT SIDE:** WSF, rejoin yarn at neck edge, pick up sts from holder and work as for left side from * to end.

Front

Work as for back to *** then cont

straight in st st and when work measures 19cm(7½ins) from beg, ending with a WSR, divide for **FRONT OPENING:** K21sts and leave on a holder and cont on rem sts for left side of work. **LEFT SIDE:** Cont straight in st st and when work measures same as back to armhole, ending with a RSR, **SHAPE ARMHOLE** as for one side of back = 17sts. Cont straight and when work measures 42cm(16½ins) from beg, ending with a WSR, **SHAPE NECK:** Cast off 5sts at beg of next row, 2sts at same edge of foll alt row, then 1 st on foll alt row = 9sts. Work 3 rows then cast off rem sts for shoulder. **RIGHT SIDE:** WSF, rejoin yarn at neck edge, pick up sts from holder and work as for left side, rev shapings.

Sleeves

Both Alike

Using 5,5mm needles cast on 28sts and cont in st st, inc 1 st at each end of every foll 4th row 3 times, then every foll 6th row 2 times = 38sts. Cont straight and when work measures 15cm(6ins) from beg ending with a WSR, **SHAPE TOP:** Cast off 2sts at beg of next 2 rows, 1 st at beg of foll 4 rows, 2 sts at beg of foll 4 rows, then 3 sts at beg of foll 2 rows = 16sts. Cast off all sts.

To Make Up

Block pieces to measurement, cover with a damp cloth and allow to dry. Sew shoulder seams.   Set in sleeves. Sew up side and sleeve seams. Sew cast on edge of sleeves closed to form end of paw. Sew crotch seam along the shaped edges at centre back and front, then sew inner leg seams. **FEET:** Sew centre back seam. Sew sole (RS to inside) into position at base of foot. Sew feet to bottom of legs, easing foot to fit. **NECKBAND:** RSF, using 5mm needles, pick up and k12sts around neck opening of left front, 16sts around back neck and 12sts around neck opening of right front = 40sts. Work in rib patt for 3cm(1in) ending with a WSR, cast off all sts loosely RW. Sew in zip to front opening.

Mac and Tosh

Basic Bear

Head, body, arms and legs worked as for bear pattern OSCAR but using 3,25mm needles and A throughout.

Ears

For both bears
Work as for bear pattern OSCAR, but make 2 pieces in A and 2 pieces in B (see picture).

Soles

Work as for bear pattern OSCAR using B (see picture).

Cardigan For Tosh

Back

Using 4mm needles cast on 52sts and k 4 rows (1st row = WS), inc 3sts evenly across last row = 55sts. Cont straight in st st, beg with a p row, and when work measures 16cm(6½ins) from beg ending with a WSR, **SHAPE NECK: Next row:** K20sts, turn. Cont on these 20sts. Dec 1 st at neck edge of next 2 rows = 18sts. Work one row, then cast off loosely. Slip next 15sts onto a stitch holder. RSF, rejoin yarn to rem sts and k to end. Cont on these 20sts. Dec 1 st at neck edge of next 2 rows = 18sts. Work one row, then cast off loosely.

Left Front

Using 4mm needles cast on 26sts. K 4 rows (1st row = WS), inc 1 st in centre of last row = 27sts. Cont straight in st st (beg with a p row) until there are 15 rows less than back to cast off edge, thus ending with a k row**. **SHAPE NECK:** Cast off 4sts at beg of next row = 23sts. Dec 1 st at neck edge of next and foll alt rows until 18sts rem. Work 3 rows, then cast off loosely.

Right Front

Work as for left front to **, but work 1 row less, thus ending with a WSR. **SHAPE NECK:** Cast off 4sts at beg of next row = 23sts. Dec 1 st at neck edge of every foll alt row until 18sts rem. Work 3 rows, then cast off loosely.

Sleeves

Both Alike

Using 3,25mm needles cast on 41sts and work 6 rows in g st (see general instructions) inc 2sts evenly across last row = 43sts. Change to 4mm needles and cont in st st (beg with a p row), inc 1 st at each end of every foll 4th row until there are 51sts. Cont straight until work measures 9cm(3½ins) from beg, ending with a WSR, then cast off loosely.

To Make Up

Block pieces to measurement, cover with a damp cloth and allow to dry. Sew shoulder seams. **NECKBAND:** RSF, using 4mm needles pick up and k 50sts evenly around neck including sts from stitch holder. K 3 rows, then cast off loosely kw. **RIGHT FRONT BAND:** RSF, using 4mm needles pick up and k 36sts evenly along edge of right front and across edge of neckband. K 1 row. **Next row, buttonhole row:** K2sts, (yfd, k2tog, k4sts) 5 times, yfd, k2tog, k2sts (= 6 buttonholes). K 1 row, then cast off loosely. **LEFT FRONT BAND:** Work as for right front band omitting buttonholes. ****Place markers 10cm on either side of shoulder seams. Set in sleeves between markers. Sew up side and sleeve seams. Sew on buttons**.** Swiss darn (see general instructions) initial in centre of right front panel (see chart and picture).

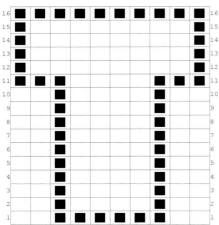

Pullover For Mac

Back And Sleeves

Work as for cardigan for Tosh.

Front

Work as for back of cardigan and when work is 15 rows less than back to cast off edge ending with a WSR, **SHAPE NECK:** K23sts and leave on a holder, cast off centre 9sts and cont on rem sts for left side of work. **LEFT SIDE:** Work one row. **Cast off 1 st at beg (neck edge) of next and every foll alt row 5 times in all = 18sts. Work 3 rows, then cast off loosely. **RIGHT SIDE:** WSF, rejoin yarn at neck edge, pick up sts from holder and work as for left side from ** to end.

To Make Up

Block pieces to measurement, cover with a damp cloth and allow to dry. Sew right shoulder seam. **NECKBAND:** RSF, using 3,25mm needles, pick up and k50sts all round neck edge including sts from holder. K 3 rows, then cast off loosely kw. Catch the two shoulder seams together at shoulder edge. Work one row dc across shoulder openings working 3 button loops evenly across back shoulder edge. Complete as for cardigan from ** to **. Swiss darn (see general instructions) initial in centre of front (see chart and picture).

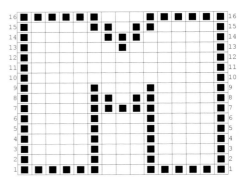

MAC AND TOSH

Cuddles

MATERIALS:
ALASKA AND CHUNKY
CUDDLES: 250g Stone CHUNKY
One pair 16mm black glass eyes.
One 30mm black plastic nose.
Baby's dummy and nappy.
Oddments of black yarn for embroidery.
Polyester stuffing.
One pair 4,5mm knitting needles.
BABY GROW: 250g White ALASKA
One 30cm(11¾ins) zip.
One pair each 5mm and 5,5mm knitting needles.
Stitch holders.

MEASUREMENTS:
Cuddles measures 40cm(15¾ins) sitting and 60cm(23½ins) standing.
Baby Grow:
Actual all round measurement:
Chest: 60cm(23½ins)
Length to back neck: 45cm(17¾ins)
Sleeve seam: 15cm(6ins)

TENSION:
SAVE TIME, TAKE TIME, CHECK TENSION.
BEAR: 18sts and 26 rows = 10cm(4ins) over stocking stitch using 4,5mm needles and Chunky.
BABY GROW: 14sts and 19 rows = 10cm(4ins) over stocking stitch using 5,5mm needles and Alaska.

Basic Bear

Work as for bear pattern OSCAR but using 4,5mm needles throughout.

Baby Grow

Feet

Both Alike
Using 5,5mm needles, cast on 52sts and work in st st for 5 rows. **SHAPE FOOT:** P24sts, (p2tog) twice, p24sts = 50sts. Work 3 rows st st. P23sts, (p2tog) twice, p23sts = 48sts. Work 3 rows st st. P20sts, (p2tog) 4 times, p20sts = 44sts. K20sts, (k2tog) twice, k20sts = 42sts. P15sts, (p2tog) 6 times, p15sts = 36sts. K one row. P14sts, (p2tog) 4 times, p14sts = 32sts. K one row. P14sts, (p2tog) twice, p14sts = 30sts. Inc 7sts evenly across next and foll row = 44sts. Cast off all sts loosely.

Soles

Make two soles as for bear pattern OSCAR but using 5,5mm needles.

Back

FIRST LEG: Using 5,5mm needles cast on 24sts for lower edge of leg and cont straight in st st for 12cm(4¾ins) ending with a RSR**, cast off 1 st at beg of next row = 23sts. K one row. Cut yarn and leave these sts on a holder. **SECOND LEG:** Work as for first leg to **. P one row. Cast off 1 st at beg of next row. Now join the 2 legs by working across all sts as folls:- **Next row:** P23sts of second leg then p23sts of first leg = 46sts. **Next row:** K21sts, k2tog, SKPO, k21sts. **Next row:** P. **Next row:** K20sts, k2tog, SKPO, k20sts = 42sts***. Cont straight in st st and when work measures 30cm(11¾ins) from beg, ending with a WSR, **SHAPE ARMHOLES:** Cast off 2sts at beg of next 2 rows, then 1 st at beg of foll alt row 4 times in all = 34sts. Cont straight and when work measures 45cm(17¾ins) from beg, ending with a WSR, **SHAPE NECK:** K11sts and leave on a holder, cast off centre 12sts and cont on rem sts for left side of work. **LEFT SIDE:** Work one row. *Dec 1 st at beg (neck edge) of next 2 rows = 9sts. Cast off rem sts for shoulder. **RIGHT SIDE:** WSF, rejoin yarn at neck edge, pick up sts from holder and work as for left side from * to end.

Front

Work as for back to *** then cont straight in st st and when work measures 19cm(7½ins) from beg, ending with a WSR divide for **FRONT OPENING:** K21sts and leave on a holder and cont on rem sts for left side of work. **LEFT SIDE:** Cont straight in st st and when work measures same as back to armhole, ending with a RSR, **SHAPE ARMHOLE** as for one side of back = 17sts. Cont straight and when work measures 42cm(16½ins) from beg, ending with a WSR, **SHAPE NECK:** Cast off 5sts at beg of next row, 2sts at same edge of foll alt row, then 1 st

on foll alt row = 9sts. Work 3 rows then cast off rem sts for shoulder. **RIGHT SIDE:** WSF, rejoin yarn at neck edge, pick up sts from holder and work as for left side, rev shapings.

Sleeves

Both Alike
Using 5,5mm needles cast on 28sts and cont in st st, inc 1 st at each end of every foll 4th row 3 times, then every foll 6th row 2 times = 38sts. Cont straight and when work measures 15cm(6ins) from beg ending with a WSR, **SHAPE TOP:** Cast off 2sts at beg of next 2 rows, 1 st at beg of foll 4 rows, 2 sts at beg of foll 4 rows, then 3 sts at beg of foll 2 rows = 16sts. Cast off all sts.

Hood

Using 5,5mm needles cast on 51sts for front edge and work in g st for 5cm(2ins) ending with a WSR. **OPENING FOR EARS:** K6sts, cast off 14sts, k11sts, cast off 14sts, k6sts. **Next row:** K6sts, cast on 14sts, k11sts, cast on 14sts, k6sts = 51sts. Now cont straight in st st for 8 rows, **SHAPE NECK EDGES:** Dec 1 st at each end of next row, then on foll 8th row once and foll 6th row twice = 43sts. Work 2 rows. Cast off 5sts at beg of next 4 rows = 23sts. Cast off all sts.

To Make Up

Block pieces to measurement, cover with a damp cloth and allow to dry. Sew shoulder seams. Set in sleeves. Sew up side and sleeve seams. Sew cast on edge of sleeves closed to form paw. Sew crotch seam along the shaped edges at centre back and front then sew inner leg seams. **FEET:** Sew centre back seam. Sew sole (RS to inside) into position at base of foot. Sew feet to bottom of legs, easing foot to fit. Sew back hood seam along cast off edges then sew neck edges of hood to neck edges of back and front, easing in hood to fit. Sew in zip to front opening. Make a pom-pom and attach to hood (see picture).

CUDDLES

CUDDLES

Little Love Bear

MATERIALS:
CAPRI AND FAMILY KNIT DK
CAPRI: 50g Rich Cream A.
FAMILY KNIT DK: 50g Antique B.
One pair 8mm smokey topaz glass eyes.
One 24mm black plastic nose.
Oddments of black yarn for embroidery.
3 Gold fabric hearts.
Polyester stuffing.
One pair 3mm knitting needles.

MEASUREMENTS:
Little Love Bear measures 18cm(7ins) sitting and 25cm(9¾ins) standing.

TENSION:
SAVE TIME, TAKE TIME, CHECK TENSION.
24sts and 34 rows = 10cm(4ins) over stocking stitch using 3mm needles.

Body

Using 3mm needles and A, cast on 18sts.
1st row: K.
2nd row: P, inc into first 2sts, p5sts, inc into next 4sts, p5sts, inc into last 2sts = 26sts.
3rd row: K, inc into first st, k10sts, inc into next 4sts, k10sts, inc into last st = 32sts.
4th row: P, inc into first st, p14sts, inc into next 2sts, p14sts, inc into last st = 36sts.
5th row: K, inc 1 st at each end of row = 38sts.
6th row: P18sts, inc into next 2sts, p18sts = 40sts.
7th row: K, inc 1 st at each end of row = 42sts.
8th row: P20sts, inc into next 2sts, p20sts = 44sts.
9th to 16th row: Work in st st.
17th row: K2tog, k18sts, (k2tog) twice, k18sts, k2tog = 40sts.
18th row: P.
19th row: K18sts, (k2tog) twice, k18sts = 38sts.
20th and 21st row: Work in st st.
22nd row: P17sts, (p2tog) twice. p17sts =38sts.
23rd row: K.
24th row: P16sts, (p2tog) twice, p16sts = 34sts.
25th row: K.
26th row: P15sts, (p2tog) twice, p15sts = 32sts.
27th row: K14sts, (k2tog) twice, k14sts = 30sts.
28th row: P13sts, (p2tog) twice, p13sts = 28sts.
29th and 30th row: Work in st st.
31st row: K12sts, (k2tog) twice, k12sts = 26sts.
32nd row: P.
33rd row: K, inc into first st, k10sts, (k2tog) twice,k10sts, inc into last st = 26sts.
34th and 35th row: Work in st st.
36th row: P11sts, (p2tog) twice, p11sts = 24sts.
37th row: K, dec 1 st (=work 2tog) at each end of row = 22sts.
38th row: P2tog, p7sts, (p2tog) twice, p7sts, p2tog = 18sts.
39th row: (K2tog) 9 times = 9sts. Cast off.

Head

Using 3mm needles and A, cast on 29sts.
1st row: K.
2nd row: P, inc 1 st at each end of row = 31sts.
3rd and 4th row: Cast on 8sts at beg of each row = 47sts.
5th row: K18sts, inc into next st, k9sts, inc into next st, k18sts = 49sts.
6th row: P.
7th row: K, inc 1 st at each end of row = 51sts.
8th to 11th row: Work in st st.
12th row: P20sts, inc into next st, p9sts, inc into next st, p20sts = 53sts.
13th row: K.
14th and 15th row: Cast off 4sts at beg of each row = 45sts.
16th and 17th row: Cast off 6sts at beg of each row = 33sts.
18th row: P2tog, p10sts, inc into next st, p7sts, inc into next st, p10sts, p2tog = 33sts.
19th row: K.
20th row: P9sts, p2tog, p11sts, p2tog, p9sts = 31sts.
21st row: K2tog, k6sts, k2tog, k11sts, k2tog, k6sts, k2tog = 27sts.
22nd row: P, dec 1 st (= work 2tog) at each end of row = 25sts.
23rd row: K2tog, k1 st, (k2tog) twice, k11sts, (k2tog) twice, k1 st, k2tog = 19sts.
24th row: Cast off 4sts at beg of row, inc into next st, then p to end = 16sts.
25th row: Cast off 4 sts at beg of row, inc into next st, then k to end = 13sts.
26th to 32nd row: Work in st st.
33rd row: K, dec 1 st at each end of row = 11sts.
34th and 35th row: Work in st st.
36th row: P, dec 1 st at each end of row = 9sts.
37th and 38th row: Work in st st.
39th row: K, dec 1 st at each end of row = 7sts.
40th to 52nd row: Work in st st.
53rd row: K, dec 1 st at each end of row = 5sts.
54th row: P.
Cast off all sts.

Ears

Make 2 pieces in A and 2 pieces in B
Using 3mm needles cast on 11sts.

1st to 3rd row: Work in st st.
4th to 6th row: Dec 1 st at each end of every row = 5sts.
7th row: K2tog, k1 st, k2tog = 3sts.
8th row: P3tog, fasten off.

Arms

Make 2

Using 3mm needles and A, cast on 4sts.
1st row: K.
2nd row: P, inc into every st = 8sts.
3rd row: K, inc into first st, k2sts, inc into next 2sts, k2sts, inc into last st =12sts.
4th row: P, inc 1 st at each end of row = 14sts.
5th row: K, inc into first st, k5sts, inc into next 2sts, k5sts, inc into last st = 18sts.
6th row: P, inc 1 st at each end of row = 20sts.
7th row: K8sts, (k2tog) twice, k8sts = 18sts.
8th row: P, inc into first st, p6sts, (p2tog) twice, p6sts, inc into last st = 18sts.
9th row: K7sts, (k2tog) twice, k7sts = 16sts.
10th row: P6sts, (p2tog) twice, p6sts = 14sts.
11th row: K, inc into first st, k4sts, (k2tog) twice, k4sts, inc into last st = 14sts.
12th row: P5sts, (p2tog) twice, p5sts = 12sts.
13th to 17th row: Work in st st.
18th row: P, inc 1 st at each end of row =14sts.
19th to 34th row: Work in st st.
35th row: K2tog, k3sts, (k2tog) twice, k3sts, k2tog =10sts.
36th row: P.
37th row: K2tog, k1 st, (k2tog) twice, k1 st, k2tog = 6sts.
38th row: (P2tog) 3 times = 3sts.
Cast off all sts.

Legs

Make 2

Using 3mm needles and A, cast on 30sts.
1st to 8th row: Work in st st.
9th row: K13sts, (k2tog) twice, k13sts = 28sts.
10th row: P6sts, (p2tog) 8 times, p6sts = 20sts.
11th row: K2sts, (k2tog) 8 times, k2sts = 12sts.
12th and 13th row: Work in st st.
14th row: P5sts, inc into next 2sts, p5sts = 14sts.
15th to 17th row: Work in st st.
18th row: P6sts, inc into next 2sts, p6sts = 16sts.
19th to 21st row: Work in st st.
22nd row: P7sts, inc into next 2sts, p7sts =18sts.
23rd to 28th row: Work in st st.
29th row: K7sts, (k2tog) twice, k7sts = 16sts.
30th to 32nd row: Work in st st.
33rd row: K2tog, k4sts, (k2tog) twice, k4sts, k2tog = 12sts.
34th row: P2tog, p2sts, (p2tog) twice, p2sts, p2tog = 8sts.
35th row: (K2tog) 4 times = 4sts.
Cast off all sts.

Soles

Make 2

Begin at toe.
Using 3mm needles and B, cast on 4sts.
1st row: K.
2nd row: P, inc into every st = 8sts.
3rd and 4th row: Work in st st.
5th row: K, inc 1 st at each end of row = 10sts.
6th to 11th row: Work in st st.
12th row: P, dec 1 st (= work 2tog at each end of row = 8sts.
13th to 16th row: Work in st st.
17th row: K, dec 1 st at each end of row= 6sts.
18th row: P

19th row: K, dec 1 st at each end of row = 4sts.
20th row: (P2tog) twice = 2sts.
21st row: K2tog, fasten off.

To Make Up

Sew all pieces using back stitch (see general instructions). **BODY:** With right sides to inside sew back seam closed leaving an opening for stuffing. Stuff firmly and ladder stitch (see general instructions) the gap closed. **HEAD:** With right sides to inside sew side seams of head gusset (see diagram 1 on page 12), then muzzle seam (see diagram 2), leaving neck (cast on edge) open. If nose and eyes need to be attached before stuffing, do so now (see general instructions). Stuff head and nose firmly. Using a new thread, run a gathering stitch around neck (cast on edge) at head and pull in tightly. Fasten off. Pin head to body ensuring nose seam and centre front of body are in line. Sew head firmly to body by pressing head down onto the body and sewing, making sure that the head remains straight on the body. The firmer you press the head onto the body, the more stable the head will be. **EARS:** With right sides to inside sew curved edge leaving cast on edge open. Sew closed using ladder stitch. Pin to head in desired position. Sew firmly to head ensuring neat edges. **LEGS:** Fold in half with right sides to inside and sew seams leaving an opening for stuffing. Sew sole (RS to inside) into position at base of foot (remember, cast on edge for toe). Turn right side out and stuff legs and feet firmly. Close opening. Little Love Bear's legs are movable, see general instructions for attaching legs to body. **ARMS:** Fold in half with right sides to inside and sew seams leaving an opening for stuffing. Turn right side out and stuff firmly. Close opening. The arms are also movable, see general instructions for attaching arms to body. Embroider mouth (see general instructions). Attach gold hearts.

LITTLE LOVE BEAR

Big Ben

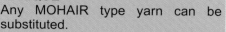

MATERIALS:
AFRIQUE
Any MOHAIR type yarn can be substituted.
550g Caramel
One pair of 22mm amber plastic eyes.
One plastic 30mm black plastic nose.
Length of ribbon.
Oddments of black yarn for embroidery.
Polyester stuffing.
One pair 6mm knitting needles.

MEASUREMENTS:
Big Ben measures 85cm(33½ins) standing.

TENSION:
SAVE TIME, TAKE TIME, CHECK TENSION.
(Using 2 strands of yarn tog): 13sts and 18 rows = 10cm(4ins) over reversed stocking stitch using 6mm needles.

Head

Make 1

Using 6mm needles and double strand, cast on 59sts and work in rev st st (see general instructions), inc 1 st at each end of next and every foll alt row 9 times in all = 77sts. Mark last row with a coloured thread on each side. Now dec 1 st (= work 2tog) at each end of next and every foll row 22 times in all = 33sts. Dec 1 st at each end of every row 15 times = 3sts. Cast off.

Ears

Make 2

Using 6mm needles and double strand, cast on 16sts and work 12 rows in rev st st. Dec 1 st at each end of foll 3 rows = 10sts. Now inc 1 st at each end of foll 3 rows = 16sts. Work 12 rows rev st st. Cast off.

Body

Make 2

Using 6mm needles and double strand, cast on 33sts and work in rev st st, inc 1 st at each end of next and every foll row 6 times in all = 45sts. Cont straight until work measures 34cm(13½ins) from beg ending with a WSR. Now dec 1 st (= work 2tog) at each end of next and every foll row 6 times in all = 33sts. Cast off.

Legs

Make 2

Using 6mm needles and double strand, cast on 23sts and work in rev st st, inc 1 st at each end of next and every foll alt row 9 times in all = 41sts. Cont straight and when work measures 30cm(11¾ins) from beg ending with a WSR. **SHAPE LEG:** Dec 1 st (= work 2tog) at each end of next and every foll row 4 times in all = 33sts. Cast off .

Arms

Make 2

Work as for legs for 26cm(10¼ins) ending with a WSR, **SHAPE ARM:** Dec 1 st at each end of next and every foll row 6 times in all = 29sts.

To Make Up

With right sides to inside, sew body pieces tog leaving an opening for stuffing. Turn to right side and stuff (lightly), sew opening closed. **ARMS AND LEGS:** With right sides to inside sew seams including shaping, leaving cast off edge open. Turn to RS and stuff leaving tops open. To attach arms and legs, pin in position with leg seams facing backwards and arm seams to underarms. Sew firmly in place inserting extra stuffing if necessary (see picture). **SHAPE**

FOOT: Run a gathering thread across front half of bottom leg and pull firmly to shape foot (see picture). **HEAD:** Place coloured threads tog and sew seams to form muzzle, then sew nose seam leaving neck open. Attach eyes and nose and stuff head. Gather around neck (cast on edge) of head and pull in tightly. Fasten off. **SHAPE NOSE:** Run a gathering thread in a circle (diameter of ±7cm) around point of nose (see diagram). Pull firmly to form nose shape, fasten off (see picture). With right sides to inside fold ears in half with cast on and cast off edges together. Sew side seams, turn right side out and ladder stitch opening closed. Attach ears to head. Pin head in position on body and attach firmly. Embroider mouth. Tie ribbon around neck.

Nose Shaping

Foot Shaping

BIG BEN

Titch

MATERIALS:
4 PLY
25g each Sunset, Tiger Lime, Royal, Tiger Cerise, Bright Yellow, Bright Red, Violet and Magenta.
One pair 12mm green glass eyes.
One 22mm black plastic nose.
Length of ribbon.
Oddments of black yarn for embroidery.
Polyester stuffing.
One pair 2,75mm knitting needles.

MEASUREMENTS:
Titch measures 24cm(9½ins) sitting and 35cm(13¾ins) standing.

TENSION:
SAVE TIME, TAKE TIME, CHECK TENSION.
34sts and 42 rows = 10cm over stocking stitch using 2,75mm needles.

Basic Bear

Work as for bear pattern OSCAR but using 2,75mm needles throughout.

Work colours as folls:
HEAD: Tiger Lime
BODY: Sunset
ARM: Bright Red
ARM: Royal
LEGS: Violet
SOLES: Magenta
EARS: 2 pieces in Bright Yellow and 2 pieces in Tiger Cerise.

Mittsy

Basic Bear

Head and ears, work as for bear pattern OSCAR.

Body

BACK AND FRONT

Both Alike

Using 3,75mm needles and A, cast on 40sts.
1st to 4th row: Work in rib patt. Now cont straight in st st until work measures 15cm(6ins) from beg ending with a WSR.
ARMS: Next 5 rows: Inc 1 st at each end of every row = 50sts.
Next 6 rows: Work in st st.
Next 5 rows: Dec 1 st (= work 2tog) at each end of every row = 40sts.
Next 2 rows: Cast off 13sts at beg of each row = 14sts.
Next 6 rows: Work in st st.
Next 8 rows: Dec 1 st at beg of every row = 6sts.
Cast off.

Paws

BACK AND FRONT
Make 2 pieces in A and B
Starting at wrist, using 3,75mm needles cast on 14sts.
1st and 2nd row: Work in st st.
3rd to 7th row: Inc 1 st at each end of next and every foll alt row = 20sts.
8th to 12th row: Work in st st.
13th to 16th row: Dec 1 st at each end of every row = 12sts.
Cast off.

To Make Up

Sew all pieces together using back stitch (see general instructions).
BODY: RS to inside sew all around seams leaving cast on edge open.
HEAD: RS to inside, sew side seams of head gusset, then muzzle seam, leaving neck (cast on edge) open. If nose and eyes need to be attached do so now. Stuff head and nose firmly. **SEW**

HEAD TO BODY: Using a thread gather around neck (cast on edge) of head, pull tightly and fasten off leaving a small opening for fingers. In order to position head on body correctly, insert neck section of body into head opening, pin in place and sew firmly all round head. The firmer you press the head onto the body, the more stable the head will be. **PAWS:** Sew front and back pieces together, leaving wrist edges open, stuff lightly. In order to position paws on body correctly, insert arm section of body into paw opening, pin in place and sew firmly all round paw. Embroider 4 evenly spaced straight stitches on each paw for claws. **EARS:** RS to inside, sew curved edge leaving cast on edge open. Turn to right side and stuff ears lightly, sew closed using ladder stitch (see general instruction). Pin to head in desired position and sew in place. Embroider mouth (see general instructions). Sew on buttons.

MITTSY

53

Saffron

Basic Bear

Work as for bear pattern OSCAR but using 4mm needles throughout. Work soles in B. Ears, work 2 pieces in A and 2 pieces in B.

Pullover

Back

Using 4mm needles and A, cast on 57sts and work 6 rows in rib patt (see general instructions). Cont straight in st st and when work measures 12cm(4¾ins) from beg ending with a WSR, **DIVIDE FOR BACK OPENING:** K28sts and leave on a holder, cast off 1 st and cont on rem sts for left side of work. **LEFT SIDE:** **Cont straight in st st and when work measures

18cm(7ins) from beg ending at neck edge, **SHAPE NECK:** Cast off 8sts at beg (neck edge) of next row and 1 st at same edge of foll 2 alt rows = 18sts. Work one row, then cast off loosely. **RIGHT SIDE:** WSF, rejoin yarn at neck edge, pick up sts from holder and work as for left side from ** to end.

Front

Work as for back omitting back opening and when work is 10 rows shorter than back to shoulder, ending with a WSR, **SHAPE NECK:** K23sts, leave on a holder, cast off centre 11sts and cont on rem sts for left side of work. **LEFT SIDE:** Work one row. **Cast off 1 st at beg (neck edge) of next and every foll alt row 5 times in all = 18sts. Cont straight and when work measures same as back to shoulder, ending with a WSR, cast off all sts loosely. **RIGHT SIDE:** WSF, rejoin yarn at neck edge, pick up sts from holder and work as for left side from ** to end.

Lazy Daisy Stitch

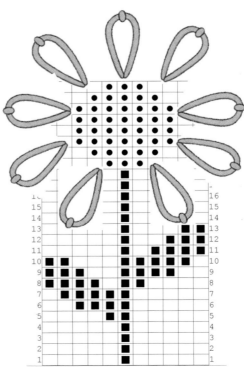

Sleeves

Both Alike
Using 4mm needles and A, cast on 42sts and work 6 rows in rib patt. Change to 4mm needles and cont in st st inc 1 st at each end of every foll 4th row 5 times = 52sts. Cont straight until work measures 14cm(5½ins) from beg ending with a WSR, cast off loosely.

To Make Up

Block pieces to measurement, cover with a damp cloth and allow to dry. Sew shoulder seams. **NECKBAND:** RSF, using 4mm needles and A, pick up and k12sts up left back neck, 24sts around front neck opening and 12sts down right back neck = 48sts. Work in rib patt for 4cm(1½ins) ending with a WSR, then cast off loosely RW. Place markers 12cm(4¾ins) on either side of shoulder seams. Set in sleeves between markers. Sew up side and sleeve seams. Work one row dc around neckband and back opening. Sew on press studs. Swiss darn (see general instructions) flower in centre of front beginning stem on first row of st st above rib. Then using lazy daisy stitch (see diagram) and double strand of yarn, work petals alternating in B and C. Work one row chain stitch around centre of flower using C.

SAFFRON

Teddy Bears Picnic

MATERIALS:
FAMILY KNIT 4 PLY, DK AND CHUNKY

DADDY BEAR: ✳
250g CHUNKY colour of your choice
One pair 16mm black glass eyes
One 30mm black plastic nose
One pair 4,5mm knitting needles

MOMMY BEAR: ✳
150g DOUBLE KNIT colour of your choice
One pair 12mm smokey topaz glass eyes
One 25mm black plastic nose
One pair 3mm knitting needles

BABY BEAR: ☆
100g 4 PLY colour of your choice
One pair 12mm light blue glass eyes
One 16mm black flocked nose
One pair 2,75mm knitting needles
Length of ribbon for each bear
Polyester stuffing for each bear
Oddments of black yarn for embroidery

MEASUREMENTS:
Daddy bear measures 40cm(15¾ins) sitting and 60cm(23½ins) standing.
Mommy bear measures 30cm(11¾ins) sitting and 46cm(18ins) standing.
Baby bear measures 24cm(9½ins) sitting and 35cm(13¾ins) standing.

TENSION:
SAVE TIME, TAKE TIME, CHECK TENSION.
Daddy bear: 18sts and 26 rows = 10cm(4ins) over stocking stitch using 4,5mm needles and Chunky.
Mommy bear: 26sts and 36 rows = 10cm(4ins) over stocking stitch using 3mm needles and Double Knit.
Baby bear: 34sts and 42 rows = 10cm(4ins) over stocking stitch using 2,75mm needles and 4 Ply.

All Bears

Work as for basic pattern OSCAR but using required needles throughout.

Acknowledgments

There are many people who have contributed in a very special way to the creation of this book.

Firstly my team; the girls in the Saprotex Design Studio. The studio is a very special place, not only because of each girl's varied talents, but more specifically for the raw creativity and enthusiasm that abounds with each project we undertake. This is evident in our book. We had great fun creating all the different bears, naming them, giving them personalities, creating settings for each photo shoot and finally, compiling the book. My grateful thanks to a talented crew; **Linda Mynhardt** and **Marelie Hurter** - designers and pattern writers; **Jolene Botha** - set designer and **Tracey Barratt** our Design Studio co-ordinator who works quietly in the background, helping the creative people to create.

Our knitters; Elsa Clack, Jean Farrer, Karen Ferreira, Charmaine Hensberg, Judy Martin, Mattie Mathee and Joan Retief. Thank you so much for the beautiful knitting of our family of bears and for meeting our tough deadlines with a smile.

Our photographer **Rob Pollock**, an integral member of our team, always happy, always striving for the best possible shot, always going the extra mile...thank you Rob.

Praise and thanks go to **Les Martens** and his team at Unifoto International. This company continually rises to the challenge of great service. Their deadlines are horrendous but still they meet the challenge, go the extra mile and deliver on time...thank you, Les.

A special thank you to Manniken Bears for loaning us the beautiful range of furniture and accessories that you see in various photographs, and to Mr Mike Cloran for allowing us the use of his painting as a background for Blue on page 24.

Another big thank you to the following companies in East London who have allowed us to use items from their stores as props in our photographs.

Exclusive Books,
Vincent Park Centre,
East London.
Tel: +27 43 726 3200

Floradale Nurseries,
East London.
Tel: +27 43 748 2420

Magnum Interiors,
25 Patterson Street,
East London.
Tel: +27 43 722 3030

Slater's Toy Magic,
Berea Mall,
Chamberlain Rd,
Berea,
East London.
Tel: +27 43 726 5762

Spargs Home and Leisure,
The Bay, Major Square,
Beacon Bay,
East London.
Tel: +27 43 748 2435

Woolworths,
Vincent Park Centre,
East London.
Tel: +27 43 726 8790

Berea Pharmacy,
31 Pearce Street,
East London.
Tel: +27 43 721 1300

Knitting is an exciting craft and we hope this book will help to revive a beautiful but rather neglected hobby, and that the outcome will be very many BEAUTIFUL BEARS.

Sharon Farr

List Of Suppliers

While most yarns are suitable for making knitted bears, more exotic yarns will make more exotic bears. The yarns used in this book are manufactured by Saprotex International, South Africa. For trade enquiries please contact:-

Saprotex International (Pty) Ltd
P.O. Box 1293
East London
South Africa
5200
Phone: +27 43 7631531
Fax: +27 43 7631929
Website: http://www.knit1.net

United Kingdom Distributors
Quadra (UK) Ltd
Tey Grove, Elm Lane
Feering
Essex
England
C05 9ES
Phone: +44 (0) 1376 573802
Fax: +44 (0) 1376 573801
E-mail address:
Quadrauk@aol.com

USA Distributors
Knitting Fever Inc./Euro Yarns
35 Debevoise Avenue
Roosevelt
New York
11575
Phone: +1 516 5463600
Fax: +1 516 5466871

Teddy Bear Accessories

MANNIKEN - The Teddy & Quilters' Lodge
1 Mulberry Lane
Beacon Bay
East London
South Africa
5200
Phone/Fax: +27 43 7481582
E-Mail address:
mannkin@global.co.za
Website:
http://www.mannikenbears.co.za

Cape Teddy Bear Supply Co.
18 Long Street
Mowbray
Cape Town
South Africa
7700
Phone/Fax: +27 21 6853487
E-Mail address: ebears@iafrica.com
Website:
http://users.iafrica.com/e/eb/ebears

The specifications listed below are for the Saprotex yarns used in this book. These specifications are for normal garment knitting and are shown here in order to help with yarn comparisons.
Please Note:
In order to create a tighter knitted fabric the bears in this book were knitted using smaller sized needles than is normal. This is to ensure a neat look that does not allow stuffing to show through when the bear is completed.

QUALITY	QUALITY	NEEDLES	WEIGHT
Family Knit 4 ply	26sts and 36 rows	3,25mm	Light
Mirage 4 ply	26sts and 36 rows	3,25mm	Light
Family Knit DK	22sts and 30 rows	4mm	Medium
Rustica DK	22sts and 30 rows	4mm	Medium
True Blue DK	22sts and 30 rows	4mm	Medium
Lussuria	18sts and 28 rows	4mm	Heavy Medium
Capri	20sts and 30 rows	4mm	Heavy Medium
Velluto	20sts and 28 rows	4,5mm	Heavy Medium
Fantasia	20sts and 28 rows	4,5mm	Heavy Medium
Mexican Wave Aran	17sts and 25 rows	5mm	Heavy Medium
Mohair 2000	16sts and 22 rows	5mm	Hunky
Afrique	16sts and 22 rows	5mm	Hunky
Family knit Chunky	15sts and 21 rows	5,5mm	Hunky
Alaska	14sts and 19 rows	5,5mm	Hunky

Published in 2002 by Saprotex International (Pty) Ltd
PO Box 1293, East London, 5200, South Africa.
Photography by Rob Pollock Photography
Production and Printing by Unifoto International (Pty) Ltd

ISBN 0-620-29302-0